A

Lie

Can Hurt

Dedication

I dedication this back to God who gave me the ability to put this book together. Most of all I'm thankful my Late wife Dorist L. Harris. Who stayed beside me thought it all. And my family and friends thank you for the support you guys gave me.

Stony Harris

Copyright 12/20/14
End 2/5/15
Written by Stony Harris

Hey, my name is Paul can I show how Satan (devil) don't mine use anyone. To do his dirty work so they will miss heaven.

Be sober, be vigilant; because your adversary the devil, as a roaring lion, walketh about, seeking whom he may devour:

The thief cometh not, but for to steal, and to kill, and to destroy: I am come that they might have life, and that they might have it more abundantly.

Submit yourselves therefore to God. Resist the devil, he will flee from you.

I was rise in the church as long as I can remember. Mom made sure I was there on Wednesday and Sunday. No matter what if mom had to work late.

Oh, she would call one of the Deacon come and pick me up. I couldn't hang out with my friends on church nights or call them. At first I loved going to church because I met a lot of friends there.

I used to play the drums for church on Sunday morning. Somehow when I got older I started slowly backing away from the church. Because I thought it was getting boring.

I always see the same people every Sunday. And I had to

listen to their same old testimony. How God have been good to them.

My mouth shall shew forth the righteousness and thy salvation all the day; for I know not the numbers thereof.

I will go in the strength of the Lord GOD: I will make mention of thy righteousness, even of thine only.

O God, thou hast taught me from my youth: hitherto have I declared thy wondrous works.

Now also when I am old and grayheaded, O God, forsake me not; until I have shewed the strength unto this generation, and thy power to every one that is to come.

Whosoever therefore shall confess me before men, him will I confess also before my Father which is in heaven.

So, I start to make up excuses, I won't have to go. I even got a part time job. I met a girl named Jody.

She was so beautiful, and I almost got caught up in her world. I found out she stopped going to church. And she don't praise God anymore. We became good friends that is what I thought.

Then later I found out she love to hang around bad company.

Thinking about the people around her is her friends. If something happened to her. They will be there for her.

A ma that hath friends must shew himself friendly: and there is a friend that sticketh closer than a brother.

Greater love hath no man that this, that a man lay down his life for his friends.

I tried my best to warn her about her friends. I used to tell her all the time they weren't your friends.

Pride goeth before destruction, and an haughty spirit before a fall.

Again, When a righteous man doth turn from his righteousness, and commit iniquity, and I lay a stumblingblock before him, he shall die: because thou hast not given him warning, he shall die in his sin, and his righteous which he hath done shall not be remembered; but his blood will I require at thine hand.

Nevertheless if thou warn the righteous man, that the righteous sin not, and he doth not sin, he is warned; also thou hast delivered thy soul.

Because they always get into trouble but it seem like it

doesn't bother her. I told her one day if she don't be careful it will catch up with her.

But she refused to pay me any attendance. Jody always tell me I'm different than what she love about me.

I told her it because my mom always keep me in church. So, I didn't really hang out with friends. Only at school and the people at church. And she keep a close eye on me. I couldn't get into trouble.

And if mom only knew I would try to smoke, drink and go to parties.

She would call my uncle Rob was a big man, and he didn't play. I used to hate it when mom told him. When I step out of line. He will put something on my backside. While he is doing it to me, he would quote this old to me all the time. I will never forget it either.

Withhold not correction from the child: for thou beastest him with the rod, he shall not die.

Thou shalt beat him with the rod, and shalt deliver his from soul hell.

Whatever he say you had better do it no question ask. Everyone in the family was afraid of him. So, I knew I had to watch my steps. What I meant the things I do. It will come back and hunt me later.

Be not deceived; God is not mocked: for whatsoever a man soweth, that shall he also reap.

Give, and it shall be given unto you; good measure, pressed down, and shaken together, and running over, shall men give into your bosom. For with the same measure that ye mete withal it shall be measure to you again.

And I remember what uncle told me the last time I saw him. Boy, if I hear or see you step out of line. "I will be there said Uncle Rob.

Jody is always trying to talk me into skip school with her and her friends. So, they can smoke some weed (marijuana) to get high. But I always refuse to go with them.

Her friends always say I was different. And told Jody, you shouldn't be hanging around me. Something might rub off on you. Her friends used to say nasty things to me. And threaten me to say if we catch you alone we're going to beat me up.

Sometimes they would hurt my feelings. But Jody always say don't worry about them guys. I will never forget one night, one of her friend's name Bullet. Because he had been shot before.

One Saturday night, mom finally let me go to the game. As we were all walking from a basketball game. He (Bullet) stopped and asked us do we wanted a ride home.

Everyone said yes, even Jody got into the car. I tried to stop her, but she refused to walk with me.

I started having a bad feeling about something that just isn't right. I said to myself I knew Bullet had a car in the past before.

But he don't keep it long, somehow he always end up wrecking it. So, I told him, I will walk home with the other guys who are going my way.

He yelled out of the window; I don't care anyway because I never like you. Me and the other boys keep walking.

I heard a police siren behind us and blew their horns. And they're yelling at us to move out of the street. I wondered what that was all about. All sudden a thought came to me that Bullet must have stolen the car he was driving.

Oh, no Jody was riding with him. I hope Bullet take her straight home. If he didn't maybe she going to jail tonight. I ran to her house hoping she was there. I run fast as I can.

I started seeing blue lights everywhere and my heart started pumping faster. It seemed like everything ran through my head. Jody may be in an accident or in hand cuff heading down town. I stop and close my eyes afraid to look anymore. Because of what I may see.

I peeked out of one it was a bad wreck as I walked toward it. I was praying no one in the car, or anyone got hurt.

Call unto me, and I will answer thee, and shew thee great and mighty things, which thou knowest not.

The righteous cry, and the LORD hearth, and delivereth them out of all their troubles.

Oh, wow it was that same car Bullet were driving early. I said to myself.

But I didn't see anyone in it. I ask did anyone get hurt, a man yelled no body wasn't in the car. I guess whoever was driving must have jumped out and run.

The police yelled out. Do anyone know who was driving this car? But no one answered and I dropped my head and walked away.

I finally made it to Jody's house. Hoping she would come to the door. I knocked on the door and her mother yelled, "Who is it?

I'm Paul, my friend Jody is she home?

No, she haven't made it home yet. She told me she was going to the game with some friends early. Is something wrong? She looked up at me.

Ma, I saw her at the game, we all left about the same time. I thought she would've made it home by now.

Should I call the police? she asked.

Ma, I don't know please wait maybe she will show up soon. I wanted to tell her mom that Jody were hanging out with some trouble maker friends. They isn't good for her. But just I walked away praying she was alright.

Little children, let no man deceive you: he that doeth righteousness is righteous, even as is righteous.

He that committeth sin is of the devil; for the devel sinneth from the beginning. For this purpose the Son of God was manifested, that he might destroy the works of the devil.

He that walketh with wise men shall be wise: but a

companion of fools shall be destroyed.

God from the presence of a foolish man, when thou perceivest not in him lip of knowledge.

And I'm afraid something bad is going to happen to her. If she don't stop hanging out with her friends. But I didn't want to get her in trouble with her parents.

So, I told her mother I got to go home before my mother started worrying about me. Please tell her to call me when she get home. Ma.

Okay!

Thank you and have good night.

So, I made it home and my mother was sitting at the kitchen table drinking some milk. She ask me how was the game?

It was great we won the game with a sad look on my face. Because I was worried about Jody hadn't made it home.

I heard on the news it was a bad accident. Someone stole a car and went for a joy ride. But they say no one was in it. They don't know who stolen the car yet said a police officer.

Did you hear or see anything while you were coming from

the game? Did you see the car how bad it was messed up? Mom looked up at me.

Yes, ma, matter of face I saw the police pass by me while I was walking back home.

I bet it was some young kids trying to show off. And driving fast they lost control of the car. Mom started back drinking her milk.

I didn't answer because I knew she was right. And I know who drove it too. But I was too afraid to tell mom about it.

Mom can't hold water (secret), she would've told the neighborhood. And she would've called the police to tell me what really happened.

Then I got in trouble with Jody's friends for real. I gave mom a big kiss on her cheek. And I told her I will see you Miss. Pretty in the morning.

I get into the shower. I'm so tired after it had been a long night. I'm ready for bed. I stopped and prayed for the ones who were in the car.

And call upon me in the day of trouble: I will deliver thee, and thou shalt glorify me.

And the LORD, he it is that doth go before thee, he will be with thee, he will not fail thee, neither forsake thee: fear not, neither be dismayed.

These things I have spoken unto you, that in me ye might have peace. In the world ye shall have tribulation: but be of good cheer; I have overcome the world.

So, I put on my night clothes and put my phone on the night stand. Hoping Jody would call me before I fall sleep. I just need to hear her voice. Let me know she made home and safe.

But I tried to wait for her to call. My eyes got heavy and fell to sleep. Mom ran into my room to shake me. Asking me if I was going to work this morning.

I rolled over to ask her what time it was.

It is 7:15.

Oh, Lord I'm running late, I jumped out of the bed and ran into bathroom.

I grab my uniform to throw on. And grab my tooth brush. I had better call in to let them know I'm running a little late this morning.

Mom yelled, "do you want some breakfast?

No ma, I'm already late, I better got to work before my boss coming in. I yelled back as I was running out the door. And I gave mom a kiss on her cheek.

I ran down to the bus stop and waited for the next bus to arrive. And I heard some guys talking about the wreck happening last night.

One guy said, "Did you see how bad that car was messed up? I wondered if someone got hurt.

And the other guy asked did they caught that person who did it yet?

No, I didn't think so that what the newspaper said.

Oh, wow it made the headlines and that's all I heard last night. When I was getting ready for work. I turn on the television it were on just about every channel said the one guy.

Man, that so mess up someone want to steal another person car. And turned around wreck it that so sad maybe it was a lady car who had kids. Or a man just trying to feed his family.

Now they don't have a car to take care of their business. One guy yelled out with tears in his eyes.

Yes, that could have been someone in my family.

Now they have got to go through this.

I dropped my head; I started feeling so bad. Knowing I know who the person was responsible for all this mess.

By that time my phone rang it was Jody.

Hey, Girl, I been looking for you last night. After I saw the accident. Are you okay?

Yes, I'm fine just a little sore, Bullet told me to drive last night. Because he has been drinking and sleepy.

So, I drove Bullet home first. I drop off the rest of my friends. And I was on my way back to Bullet alone. I was hoping he would be able to drive me home. Because early he was drunk (intoxication).

Woe unto them that rise up early in the morning, that they may follow strong drink; that continue night, till wine inflame them!

Woe unto them that are mighty to drink to drink wine, and men of strength to mingle strong drink:

They shall not drink wine a song; strong drink shall be bitter to them that drink it.

Wine is a mocker, strong drink is raging: and whosoever is deceived thereby is not wise.

And I didn't want him to drive us around like that. But suddenly a deer ran out of nowhere in front of the car I was alone. I tried my best to miss it too late. I crashed the car into a big tree. I was so scared. I left the car.

Mom told me that you came last night looking for me. Sorry I didn't call you to let you know what happened to me.

It okay I'm glad no one got hurt. Hey, did you know Bullet stole the car?

Oh, no my I'm in trouble. Bullet going to kill me, when I see him. Man, this isn't cool. If my parents found out it was me crashing into the car.

Knowing I don't suppose driving anybody car. Because I don't have my driver license yet. And they really going to kill me Jody started crying.

Yep, it all is on the news, and it made the front-page newspaper.

I'm so sorry I didn't listen to you last night. That is what I get trying too popular (noticed). Hoping the guys will like me. Please, please don't tell anyone what I have done.

Okay, but we have got to figure out something to keep you out of trouble.

I'm going to call Bullet and tell him about himself. I'm mad and hurt. I see you at work.

Okay, remember Paul, we can't be late the boss will have us up in the office. Explain to ourselves again why we're late.

I called Bullet but he wasn't answering his phone. I wondered why? Maybe he heard it news too. And maybe he is on the run thinking someone is going to tell him.

They saw him driving the car. He were the person who stole the car. I'm glad I took everyone home before this happened to me. I got to find him before the police caught up with him. He may give them my name to cover up what he done.

Hey, we are at work now, let's keep this on the down low (a secret).

You already know people around here love to get into other people's business.

Yep, that is true they found out this girl works on the third floor. Her husband and she got into a big fight. He came up here on the job and broke all the windows out of her car.

Oh, yea, you're right Paul I remember that too.

Hey, why are you guys whispering? Is something wrong? Wanda (Miss. Nosier) is a co-worker who is always in everybody's business.

And withal they learn to be idle, wandering about from house to house; and not only idle; but tattles also and busybodies;

speaking things which they ought not.

And that ye study to be quiet, and to do your own business, and to work with your own hands, as we commanded you;

That ye may walk honestly toward then that are without, and that ye may have lack of nothing.

Oh no, nothing is wrong here. I and Jody walked toward the breakroom.

I know you two are up to something. But if you don't want to share with me, I understand.

Did you hear about that bad car accident? Did it happen on your street close to where you live Jody?

Paul looked at Jody, yes it happened about three blocks from my house.

Oh yea, plus it was all over the news and newspaper this morning.

Did they catch that person yet?

I don't know.

But if we hear something, we will let you know Paul smiled.

That woman is so noise she should've been a new a reporter. Because she know everybody's business.

I bet she can't keep her own business straight Jody has a sad look on her. Knowing Wanda is she finds out it was her. She would spend it like wild fire.

Yep, we better get some work done before the boss comes in a bad mood this morning. Paul whispered.

Well, I will talk to you to later my friend.

My phone keeps going off but when I try answering it. No one answered it. I wondered who was trying to play this game with me. Well, I'm just going to turn it off.

So, I can get some work done. Better I better go to the bathroom before I start. Hey Paul, I think someone seemed me running from the accident.

How do you know?

I left my phone on hoping for Bullet to call me back. And it keep beeping. When I pick it up and try to answer it no one won't say anything.

I'm scared and I don't know what to think with a tremble in my voice.

Maybe Bullet friends are trying to mess with you.

So, you will be too afraid not to tell anyone. He may have stolen the car. I know it is hard but try your best to pay no attention.

Then again may not be anything but those people trying to call you spam.

Okay, Paul thank you for helping me to make sense of this nonsense. Hey, where do you want to go for lunch today. I'm buying this time Jody yelled back.

Great, I couldn't grab anything from the house. Because I was running late.

Mom woke me up because I was tired from everything that was happening late at night. Plus, I tried to stay up waiting for your phone call.

Oh, I understand, hey I'm sorry again I didn't listen to you.

It okay! Sometimes a true friend know what is best for those they care about.

A man that hath friends must shew himself friendly: and there is a friend that stick closer than a brother.

Two are better than one; because that have a good reward for their labour.

For if they fall, the one will life up his fellow: but woe to him that is alone when he falleth; for he hath not another to help him up.

Again, if two lie together, then they have heat: but how can one be warm alone?

And if one prevail against him, two shall withstand him; and a threefold cord is not quickly broken.

But I don't care where we eat.

Okay, I see you at lunch.

Girl, you had better go to work and stop all this walking around. Before someone will report you to the boss and get your butt fired. I know you need this job just like me. I don't want to see you again until lunch time.

Before we both must stay over again to make up the time. Sorry, I can't stay with you because I don't want to miss my bus. Especially on the weekend they all run at different times.

I be sitting at the bus stop forever. And I'm trying to walk home because I grabbed the wrong shoes too this morning. Plus, it is getting too cold that, you isn't having me sick I can't come to work.

No thank you.

The bell finally rang for lunch.

Let's grab my coat before Paul yelled let's go eat.

Now, we better hurry up and figure out where we going to eat. Before we both will be holding our belly for the rest of the day hungry.

You already know we have thirty minutes to eat. And sorry we don't have any more options to be late coming back for lunch. Because we already have messed that up. Paul headed for the door.

Okay, okay, it doesn't matter just how long I eat something.

I know a chicken place just around the corner. And the food is pretty good.

My parents used to take me and grandmom there after church on Sunday Jody smiled.

Oh really! You used to go to church.

Yep, you can say I lived there when I was younger. I went every Wednesday and Sunday my parents made me go.

Mom was so hard (over protection) on me. I couldn't hang out with my friends. If it was during church time. I was always in some type of youth program at the church. I was in the choir ever since I was five years old. Then I started playing the drums also.

Also, my father is a Deacon.

Likewise must the deacons, be grave, not doubletongued, not given to much wine, not greedy of filthy lucre;

Holding the mystery of the faith in a pure conscience."

And let these also first be proved; then let them use the office of a deacon, being found blameless.

Even so must their wives be grave, not slander, sober, faithful in all things.

Let the deacons be the husbands of one wife, ruling their children and their own house well.

For they have used the office of a deacon well purchase to themselves a good degree, and great boldness in the faith which is in Christ Jesus.

Take heed therefore unto yourselves, and to all the flock, over the which the Holy Ghost hath made you overseers, to feed the church of God, which he hath purchased with his own blood.

He used to tell me I won't allow you to be like the other girls. Because he didn't want me to get caught up and end up pregnant. And the baby father won't support you. Or he won't do the right things to marriage you. Or getting into drinking and smoking. Now that is another story.

So, he tried to keep me close. I couldn't make him look bad. Because other people were watching him. They expected him to set a good example for the rest of the Deacons.

Plus, he wanted me became one of God's products, so he can use me.

Oh, wow so why did you leave the church? I got tired of doing the same things. And all the girls who knew me used to call me bad names.

And accused me I was in a cult because I used to wear dresses, long stockings and big eye glasses to school. And they talk about it every day. The boys ran up to me to knock my books out of my hands thinking they were funny.

Sometimes the girls slap and spit on me because I looked different. It was torching every day; I ran into the bathroom crying. Asking God why me got to laughing of the day? I wanted so bad to fight back. But I thought about what my dad used to tell me.

''Dearly beloved, avenge not yourselves, but rather give place unto wrath: for it is written, Vengeance is mine; I will repay, saith the Lord.''

I hated going to school but my parents made me go. Even though I tried to talk to mom and dad.

How those kids were picking on me. They thought I was lying because I didn't want to go to school anymore.

But my parents refused to go to the school to talk to my teachers about it. Plus, my father was well known around town. I guess he didn't want to start any trouble in the neighborhood.

So, I got fed up and decided to be like some of the girls at school acting wild.

"When I say unto the wicked, Thou shalt surely die; and thou givest him, not warning, nor speakest to warn the wicked from his wicked way, to save his life;

the same wicked man shall die in his iniquity; but his blood will I require at thine hand."

"Yet if thou warn the wicked, and he turn not from his wickedness, nor from his wicked way, he shall die in his iniquity; but thou hast delivered thy soul."

Maybe they will stop picking on me so much. Plus, I didn't care anymore. What my parents said from this point of view is not.

"But if the wicked turn from his wickedness, and do this lawful and right, he shall live thereby."

"Yet ye say, The way of the Lord is not equal. O ye house of Isreal, I will judge you every one after his ways."

I met a friend whose name was Jane.

She used to let me borrow some clothes to change in before class started. So, I can look like I fit in with the other kids.

And mom started to let me, and Jane hang out at Jane's house after school to study what she believe. When dad work out of town.

What?

Yep, but at that time I didn't know Jane was a party animal. And I don't think her mother knew it either. I thought she was a quiet and funny person.

Until one Friday night my mom let me spend the night with Jane. And we also had basketball at school.

Plus, mom and dad wanted some time without me.

So, it worked out perfectly for me. After the game I thought we was going back to her house. But she had another plan, someone she knew told her they were having a birthday for their older brother.

They invited her and called home first told mother. We're going to hang out after the game for a little while. So, her mother agreed. And look up at me yelled at it party time.

I said what! I can't go with you. If my dad find I'm at a party with a lot of boys there. I'm in big trouble.

Plus, they will never trust me again. She begged me to go with her for an hour or so.

I gave in to her and my heart was pumping fast.

I even said a prayer to myself. Lord, please forgive me because I know I shouldn't be going to someone else's house which I don't know anybody.

So, I stayed close by the front door because I didn't know what was going on at the party. But only with my family gathering. Or someone in the church having a birthday party for their kids.

And I have never been around a lot of guys or someone drinking and smoking. So, it was fun, and I wasn't picked on for once. Or no one calls me by any name. And my dad wasn't looking over his shoulder at me.

At first a was shy and so stayed to myself but Jane assisted I meet some of her friends.

And two of her brothers. She pulled me onto the floor to dance with her. But I didn't know how to dance.

Everyone started to laugh at me. I ran off the floor with tears in my eyes. Jane big brother stopped the hold party and made everyone apologizes to me.

And he yelled if she was a friend of my sister. You will give her respect. Or we're going to have some problem. If you know what I mean. I thought he was such an amazing and sweet person.

Now that is how I met Bullet and his friends. We have been good friends ever since. Now I don't know what happened to him.

He started drinking heavily, smoking and hanging out with older guys.

Who always got into trouble with police. I tried my best to talk to him but always said he was fine. I had a strong feeling that something was going on with him wasn't right.

What do you mean?

The Bullet I used to know wasn't heavy drinking or smoking. Yes, he did these things but not every day. He always call me or stop by my house to check on me. But lately I haven't seen him until that Friday night.

He asked me to drive him home and drop Money (friend) off at home. Now he isn't answering my phone call.

Maybe you were right because he was drunk, and he didn't seem like he knew what he was doing. Hey, maybe his phone dead or he lost it last night.

What do you think I should drop by his house? Maybe I can catch him at home.

Yes, I think so.

Okay, but I don't want to go by myself. Would you go with me?

Girl, I don't know about that you know he don't like me. So, I think it best for you to go alone. Just call me when you get there. Before you leave call me. I will meet you somewhere. Then we can disgust what goes on with him.

Okay, I'm going after work. What time is 12:16. We had better go so we won't be late for work.

Thanks for the lunch.

The food was great and looking forward to coming again Paul smiled.

Oh, I told you the food was good as we walked out the door.

Someone were talking about the wreck as they was walking in. One of them stopped and looked at me with a strange look. Then they whispered something to one another.

I hope they isn't talking about me, or I hope they don't know I'm the person who were driving the car. I said to myself.

What is wrong with you? Why are you looking like you seem like a ghost?

 It was nothing just heard someone talking about the wreck.

Then they turned around and looked back at me.

Oh, child people going to talk. Because it is the biggest news happening around here in a long time. And they're surprised who would steal another person's car like that.

Let's go back to work and you need to stop all that worry so much.

Peace I leave with you, my peace I give unto you: not as the world giveth give I unto you Let not your heart be troubled, neither let it be afraid.

But seek ye first the kingdom of God, and his righteousness; and all these things shall be added into you.

Take there fore no thought for the morrow:

for the morrow shall take thought for the things of itself. Sufficient unto the day is the evil thereof.

Cast thy burden upon the LORD, and he shall sustain thee: he shall never suffer the righteous to be moved.

Yes, I will, when I find Bullet and he admit that he is the one stolen the car.

I know but in the mean while try keep to it together. You will give yourself away. And you don't want Miss. Nosier Wanda to find out she is going to spread the news around town. She is dying to find some news about you and me. And that would make her day.

You're right about as we walk back in from lunch. Everyone stopped working looked at us. While we went back to our seat. I wonder what is going on.

Why does everyone eyes on me like I did something wrong. I said to myself my heart started pounding and I was scared.

Wow, ladies this is what you got to do all day watching other people. And run back and forward tell their business to one another. I bet we all have a story to tell.

Let's start by talking about yourself first. Now who wanted to start this show off first. Hold on for a minute why are some of you dropping your head now?

So when they continued asking him, he lifted up himself, and said unto them, He that is without sin among you let him first cast a stone at her.

And again he stooped down, and wrote on the ground.

And the which heard it, being convicted by their own conscience, went out one by one beginning at the eldest, even unto the last: and Jesus was left alone and the woman in the midst.

When Jesus had lifted up himself, and saw none but the woman, he said unto her Woman, where are those thine accuser? Hath no man condemned thee?

She said, No man, Lord. And Jesus said unto her, Neither do I condemn thee: go, and sin no more.

Then spake Jesus again unto them, saying I am the light of the world: he that followeth me shall not walk in darkness, but shall have the light of life.

I thought you ladies had so much to talk about. Go tell me that I (Paul) had a serious look on my face.

Hurry up, who want to go first?

No, I'm getting tired of your selfishness for years. And been around messy people up in here. If each of you do their work like you're supposed to do maybe this company should grow.

Just the boss considered giving us a rise around here. As I was talking the Boss walked into the room. Everyone stops in their tracks.

Well, now here's your next leading person said the boss. He know how to handle business without always putting down the company.

Like it the company fault because we're not growing.

It can't run without each one doing their part as a team. Oh, I need to see you Paul before you go home today into my office.

Wow, I didn't mean go that for I looked over at Jody, but

someone had to stand up around here.

Boy, you said a mouth full. I bet they will leave us alone now. Thanks now I'm going to work.

Yep, I think that is a good idea too. It was so quiet you can hear a pin drop. Even Miss. Nosier Wanda stopped bothering me. And I wonder if the boss is really giving that position to me. Being a leading person I said to myself.

Hey, good morning, Jody, how are you doing?

Oh, I feel a little better since you told the ladies off yesterday and what about you?

I'm fine, Mom cooked last night. So, I bought lunch for us. Some baked potatoes, green beans, bar-q baby back ribs and some old-fashioned cornbread.

Oh, yea, you know I can't wait for lunch. Now you have got my belly talking.

Oh, what is it saying?

Feed me!

Both burst out laughing.

Thanks, I need that laugh. It had been a couple of days long. I wonder what is going to happen next.

Hey, did you go over to Bullet house yesterday after work?

Yes, I did but no one answered it.

Oh, that's not good now what are you going to do?

I don't know but I'm going to Jane house that is Bullet sister. Do you remember I was telling you about her.

Yes!
When I got off work today. I pray that maybe she will have some idea where I could find him. I wondered do she knew what was going on with her brother.

Now that is a good question.

The bell rang we had better go in and clock in. So, we can get this day over.

Yep, Jody I will see you in the breakroom at break.

Good morning, Paul and Jody how are you guys doing? As Wanda walked out of the breakroom.

Oh, we're doing great and you.

I'm doing wonderful but I will talk to you guys later got do some work now.

Oh, wow what got into her all suddenly? And why she is kissing up to us like that, isn't the old Wanda we know. Jody turned to look at me.

Yep, you're right, that's not her. Now I'm scared of her wondering what up too. We had better keep our eyes on her. Because we know she is an undercover snake, she will strike anytime.

For the mouth of the wicked and the mouth of the deceitful are opened against me: they have spoken against me with a lying tongue.

They compassed me about also words of hatred; and fought against me without a cause.

For my love they are my adversaries: but I give myself unto prayer.

And they have rewarded me evil for good, and hatred for my love.

Bless them with persecute you: bless, and curse not.

They have prepared a net for my steps; my soul is bowed

down: they have digged a pit before me, into the midest whereof they are fallen themselves.

Therefore if thine enemy hunger, feed him; if he thirst, give them drink: for in so doing thou shalt heap coals of fire on his head.

Rejoice not when thine enemy falleth, and let not thine heart be glad when he stumbleth:

Ye have heard that it hath been said, Thou shalt love thy neighbour, and hate thine enemy.

But I say unto you, Love your enemies, bless them that curse you, do good to them that hate you, and pray for them which despitefully use you, and persecute you;

That ye may be the children of your Father which is in heaven: for he maketh his sun to rise on the evil and on the good, and sendeth rain on the just and on the unjust.

She is the main one in everybody's business. Now she turned into an angel overnight.

Maybe the boss told them to shape up or ship out. And he was fed up with all that drama. Well, I aren't mad at them. Paul hunk up his shoulder, oh well.

Bother burst out laughing.

Girl, I hollow (talk) back at you later I get some work done. Maybe we're on that list too. So, we have been careful around here. Before we end up on the chopped block (fired).

Oh, yes! You don't have to tell me but once. She threw her hand in the air.

Okay, I can't wait to stick my mouth into that bar-q. I looked back as I walked to my desk.

As I doing my work the Boss stop by said someone been calling here looking for you. Miss Jody.

But they didn't leave a name or a call back number. When you find who keep calling here. Please tell that person to call you at your personal time.

This is a business if it an emergency that be different. If they can't get in touch with you. I will understand.

Okay, I will take care of it. Thank you for the message.

I wondered who this person is. I wish they would stop calling before I lose my job. I got to find that person soon and see what is so important.

Hey, Paul I need your help would you come here please?

Okay, let me finish this program first.

The boss just told me that someone have been calling here. And asking for me but they won't leave their name number or a message. And I don't know who would call me at my job. But only my parents if there is an emergency.

Maybe Bullet tried to call you?

Na, I don't think so in that case he know my number. Why didn't he call me on it? With a puzzle look on her face.

Well, we better find that person soon before you're out on the street.

I know that right Paul.

I can't wait until we get off work. I'm going to stop by Money (friend) house. Maybe Bullet is hiding over there. I got to think fast so this nightmare can go away. I can't take this anymore. I feel like giving up go tell the police I have done it.

''There hath no temptation taken you but such as is common to man: but God is faithful.

Who will not suffer you be tempted above that ye are able;

but will with the temptation also make a way to escape, that ye may be able to bear it."

For the last couple of nights, I can't sleep or eat when I get home.

I'm afraid the police are going to kick my parents' door down and take me to jail.

If that happen I don't think I can live with myself. And I will break my parents' heart. Plus, my parents don't know the over side of me.

What do you mean by the over side? I looked up and opened my mouth.

Oh, I still go out to parties and drink sometimes. But that is going to come to an end very soon. If I wasn't trying to show everybody I'm different.

And be not conformed to this world:

but be ye transformed by the renewing of your mind, that ye may prove what is that good, and acceptable, and perfect, will of God.

I am crucified with Christ: nevertheless I live; yet not I, but Christ liveth in me: and the life which I now live in the flesh I live by the faith of the Son of God, who loved me, and have himself for me.

And have put on the new man, which is renewed in knowledge after the image of him that created him:

When I should have been alone. And not paid them girls no attention. Thinking about it is going to make my life better.

Instead, be thankful I was different and appreciated how my parents raised me. Teaching me the one who I really need to please that God.

Durning my high school years. Just maybe I wouldn't be in this situation.

"Shew me thy ways, O LORD; thy path."

"Lead me in thy truth, and teach me: for thou art God of my salvation; on thee do I wait all the day."

"Remember, O LORD, thy tender mercies and thy loving kindnesses; for they have been ever of old."

The LORD is my light and my salvation; whom shall I fear?

The LORD is the strength of my life; of whom shall I be afraid?"

"When the wicked, even mine enemies and my foes, came upon me to eat up my flesh, they stumbled and fell."

Though an host should encamp against me, my heart shall not fear: though war should rise against me, is this will I be confident.

One thing I have desired of the LORD, that will I seek after; that I may dwell in the house of the LORD all the day of my life, to behold the beauty of the LORD, and to enquire in his temple.

Stop blaming yourself we all made some mistakes before. And probably going to make some more. Because no one perfect but God.

For all have sinned, and come short of the glory of God;

As it is written, There is none righteous, no, not one.

We can work toward being like him (God).

Put on therefore, as the elect of God, holy and beloved, bowels of mercies, kindness, humbleness of mind, meekness, longsuffering;

Forbearing one another, and forgiving one another, if any man have a quarrel against any: even as Christ forgave you, so also do ye.

And above all these things put on charity, which is the bond of perfectness.

Wherefore, my beloved brethren, let every man be swift to hear, slow to speak, slow to wrath:

For the wrath of man worketh not the righteousness of God.

If you stop and think for five minutes it can save you from lots of heart acks.

What you do I mean? Stop rushing to make any decision if you haven't taken out some time.

And really look at the hold situation before you do it.

If any of you lack wisdom, let him ask of God, that giveth to all men liberally, and upbraideth not; and it shall be given him.

Trust in the LORD with all thine heart; and lean not unto thine own understanding.

In all thy ways acknowledge him, and shall direct thy paths.

It could come back to haunt you in your future.

Be not deceived; God is not mocked: for whatsoever a man soweth, that shall her also reap.

And the king shall and say unto them, Verily I say unto you inasmuch as ye have done it unto one of the least of these my brethren, ye have done it unto me.

Yes, I see that now, Jody had tears rolling down her face. Let me run to the bathroom and clean up my face. Before these women see me.

Girl, it is good to cry sometimes. And stop worry about these women in here. I bet all of them cried before. Sometimes we allow Satan to steal our joy. That when you need to start fighting back hold your head. And you know who your God is.

He is the Rock, his work is perfect: for all his way are judgment: a God of truth and without iniquity, just and right is he.

(For the LORD thy God is a merciful God;) he will not for forsake thee, neither destroy thee, nor forget the covenant of thy father which he sware unto them.

God is not, a man, that he should lie; neither the son of

man, that he should repent: hath he said, and shall he not do it? Or hath he spoken, and shall he not make it good?

We're just getting comfort he will drop a big hammer our head, before we know it we caught up into all type of problems. Because we wasn't paying any attention to what he is setting us up for.

Then we got to clean up the mess. Paul looked at her.

Now that is how I feel. I thought I was helping my friend out that night. Because he was drinking and driving. But look what it got me maybe facing some jail time.

Look you did help somebody first think about it.

You did help Bullet, Money and many more.

What did you say that?

Because Bullet probably was too drunk, and he could've hit a person or another car. And kill somebody maybe himself. Now that what a real friends do for one another friend look out for them.

When sometimes they isn't watching themselves. But thank God you did it.

You shouldn't be feeling bad when you know in your heart you did the right thing. Sometimes that could come with a price. You did what God done for us. He allow his son Jesus to go to the cross for pay the price.

For ye are bought with a price: therefore glorify God in your body, and in your spirit, which are God's.

Who gave himself for our sins, that he might deliver us from this present evil world, according to the will of God and our Father:

Wow, I wasn't thinking like that. Thank you, I feel like God put you into my life. Show me I need to clean up my life, as I was drying my eyes.

Remember this is only a test now. Jody

Beloved, think it not strange concerning the fiery trial which is to try you, as though some strange thing happened unto you:

But the God of all grace, who hath called us unto his eternal glory by Christ Jesus, after that ye have suffered a while, make you perfect, stablish, strengthen, settle you.

Rejoicing in hope; patient in tribulation; continuing instant in prayer;

And not only so, but we glory in tribulations also: knowing that tribulations worketh patience.

And we know that all things work together for good to them that love God, to them who are the called according to his purpose. I better go back to work. As he walked back to his desk.

Okay, thank you again for being a true friend.

I better sit down and try to do some work. I jumped up everyone looked at me. All I could think of how good God to me is. And Paul just reminded me. I couldn't contain myself I had run into the bathroom.

Let everything out before I know it I was shouting (dancing), thanking, and praising God at the same.

time. It was long overdue putting God back into my life first.

By him therefore let us offer the sacrifice of praise to God continually, that is the fruit of our lips giving thanks to his name.

Make a joyful noise the LORD, all ye lands.

Serve the LORD with gladness: come before his presence with singing.

Know ye that the LORD he is God: it is he that hath made us, and not we ourselves; we are his people, and the sheep of his pasture.

Enter into his gates with thanksgiving, and into his courts with praise: be thankful unto him, and bless his name.

For the LORD is good; his mercy is everlasting; and his truth endureth to all generations.

Praise ye the LORD. O give thanks unto the LORD; for he is good: for his mercy endureth forever.

I will greatly praise the LORD with my mouth; yea I will praise him among the multitude.

Hey, someone please go check on Jody, she maybe is sick.

I go; Wanda jumped up run into the bathroom all I saw Jody was praising her tail off. Something hit me all sudden I was praising God with her.

What is going on?

Another girl ran to the bathroom to see everything was alright. Then she started yelling and hollowing Jesus' name out. And she was dancing and praising to God.

And when the day of Pentecost was fully come, they were all with one accord in one place.

And suddenly there came a sound from heaven as of a rushing mighty wind, and filled all the house where they were sitting.

And there appeared unto them cloven tongues like as of fire, and it sat upon each of them.

And they were all filled with the Holy Ghost, and began to speak with other tongues, as the Spirit gave the utterance.

Therefore being by the right hand of God exalted, and having received of the Father the promise of the Holy Ghost, he hath shed forth this, which ye now see and hear.

But the Comforter, which is the Holy Ghost, whom the Father will send in my name, he shall teach you all things, and bring all things to your remembrance, whatsoever I have said unto you.

Howbeit when he, the Spirit of truth, is come, he will guide you into all truth: for he shall not speak of himself; but whatsoever he shall hear, that shall he speak: and he will shew you things to come.

Paul what did you say to Jody now Wanda. And the other

girl they all in the bathroom praising God too.

The boss heard about it, and he walked on the floor. Hey, what, and why is no one working?

Everyone looked at Paul what did you do to these women? I just told Jody everything is going to be alright. And I just remind her who God is. She ran into the bathroom.

The boss looked at him funny someone go get the women out the bathroom right now. He said in a mean voice. Someone yelled boss you need to come and see this.

The boss started walking toward the bathroom.

And all sudden something hit him, he started to praise and screaming Jesus, Jesus. Oh, how I'm thankful.

Oh my God, Paul you really got something stirred up around here. Now the boss got his little dance on.

Everyone yelling, O wow look at the boss getting his praise on.

That day it is like everyone catch the Holy Ghost at the same time. When things slowly calm down the boss yelled "get your things ladies.

I'm home and let you all go home for the rest of the with pay. But to be ready tomorrow it will be a full day of work.

Everyone ran up to him, gave him a big hug and thanked him. And I look back yell over to Paul good job.

Hey, Jody, you turned out this place Paul smiled.

No, I didn't God did it, I need that it was building up in me for a long time. I just couldn't help myself. I'm thankful I didn't get fired.

Let's go home, girl, did you see the boss he got his praised on too.

No, are you for real?

Yep, he turned the corner walking toward the bathroom with a mad look on his face.

All sudden a girl yelled, look at the boss getting his praise on too.

Oh, wow I hope he got his break though too. I surely did.

Hey, I need to stop at my Jane (Bullet) house first. Then check with Money (friend) to what up with him?

Because he used to call me every now and then. Just check on me. But lately it's making me feel like he is trying to hide something from me. I know God got my back. I screamed as I was walking toward the clock.

Okay, I will go with you. But how do you know she is at home.

Oh, I don't know I haven't seen her since last summer at the park with her daughter.

And she was telling me Bullet isn't the same. He stayed gone for weeks at a time.

No one know his whereabouts. I couldn't believe what I was hearing because that doesn't sound like him. I think I may have Jane number let check my phone.

I used to have it if she hadn't changed her. number. Oh, here it is let me try to call her.

Hello, is this Jane?

No ma! I'm here, my daughter. She stepped out for a minute but should be back shortly.

Could I have the address there?

First, who are you? I can't make mom upset with me. Because she always tell me we shouldn't give our personal information out.

If I don't know that person don't trust them.

Thus saith the LORD; Cursed be the man that trusteth in man, and maketh flesh his arm, and whose heart departeth from LORD.

But I will tell her that you call.

So, who I'm talking too?

My name is Jody, your mom's old friend and your uncle Bullet.

Okay, are you Miss Jody who used to come to my house with my uncle.

Yes, that's me, oh you're Selma.

Yes, ma, I remember I was 5 years you used to hang out with my mom at our house. I will make sure I tell her.

Thanks.

Hey, Paul!

Huh!

That was Jane's daughter. I just talk too. She remembered me when I used to come over with her uncle. I used to bring her candy and chips sometimes.

She always wanted me to play games with her.

Your phone is ringing you better answer it might be Jane. She is trying to call you back.

Oh, okay you're right it is her.

Hey Jane, how are you doing? It had been a long time since we saw each other.

Yes I know! I'm fine, Selma told me you call early to look for me.

Yes, I did, I have been trying to call your brother.

But he isn't answering his phone.

If you have you have seen him lately.

No, I hadn't seen him since late week, and he was driving a new car. It was black and red he smelled like he had been drinking. And I as him did he bought another car, but he didn't answer me.

He stayed that night for dinner. Then he said he was going home to take a shower and lay down for a while.

Okay!

Hey, what did Bullet do now?

Oh, did you hear the car Bullet was driving were stolen. I was with him Friday night after the game.

He asked me would I drive the car and take him home first. And I took Money home.

So, I did because like you said he did smell like he been drinking. Ask I was on my way back to Bullet house. Hoping he was able to drive me home.

A deer ran out in front of me, I tried to dodge it. But I lost control of the car, and it flipped over. I ended up hitting a big tree. I was so afraid I jumped out of the car I left it.

So, the next morning, I was getting ready for work. I turned the television on it was all over the news. Saying the car was stolen and they're looking for that person who has done it. Or the person who was driving it.

Oh, wow! That is why he didn't answer me when I asked about the car. I'm sorry this happened to you. That is why I need to find Bullet to clear my name.

Because he knew it was stolen. I thought I was helping a friend out. Plus, didn't want him to get into any more troubles.

Oh, did you know this is his last time if he get into trouble again. When the police catch up with him. The Judge already told him he don't want to see him in back his courtroom again. You will be doing some jail time.

If he did he will have served three to five years in prison.

Oh, wow, no I tried to tell him that he needed to leave his trouble marker alone. Before he, get caught up in something he can't handle. And he told me, he was a big boy don't worry about him. I will be alright.

For as he thinketh in his heart, so is he: Eat and drink, saith he to thee, But his heart is not with thee.

What are we going to do now?

I don't know Jane but first we need to find him. Before the police catch up with him. To let him tell his side of the story. I guess we can meet up tomorrow after work.

Hey, call me around 4:30, we can go look for him. Maybe we can go over couple his old friend's house. And they might know where he is hiding.

Okay, I see you tomorrow, it be great to see you again.

Now you're ready to go home.

Yes!

My stomach is talking to me. And I need to eat Paul grab his jacket. And I walked toward the door.

Okay, I'm getting hungry too. So, let's go somewhere to get something to eat before we go home.

Yes, I'm ready!

I know where we can go eat in Paul licking his lip.

What, what are you waiting for to lead the way my brother.

It is about two blocks down the street called Little Pub and they sell chicken dinner and bar-q.

That sound good, I haven't any good bar-q since my crazy uncle Tony. Before he kicked the bucket three years also (die).

Oh, really!

Girl, I'm going to hook- up you then.

We finally made it there and we took a seat. Then we ordered something to eat.

Hey, Paul!

Excuse me, I'm going to the bathroom to wash my hands.

Okay!

As I walked back to my seat.

Two police walking in the door with a picture in their hands. They were showing a picture around asking questions.

My heart dropped to pant I was scared they was going to see me. So, I hurried back to the table Paul. I'm starting to feel sick can we go home now.

Oh, no this can't happen to me.

I can't get some juicy ribs for dinner. Okay, I hope mom cooks something to night. Before she goes to church it is our revival week down at the church.

Wherefore he saith, Awake thou that sleepest, and arise from the dead, and Christ shall give thee light.

But seek ye first the kingdom of God, and his righteousness; and all these things shall be added unto you.

Repent ye therefore, and be conveted, that your sins may be blotted out when the times of refreshing shall come from the presence of the Lord;

Create in me a clean heart, O God; and renew a right spirit within me.

And he shall send Jesus Christ, which before was preached unto you:

Whom the heaven must receive until the times of restation of all things which God hath spoken by the mouth of all his holy prophets since the world began.

All the ends of the world shall remember and turn unto the LORD: and all the kindred of the nation shall worship before thee.

Either I'm just having to fast and pray.

To loose the bands of wickedness, to undo the heavy burdens, and to let the oppressed go free, and that ye break every yoke?

Moreover when ye fast, be not, as the hypocrites, of a sad countenance: for they disfigure their faces, that they may appear unto men to fast. Verly I say unto you, They have their reward

.

But thou, when thou fastest, anoint thine head, and wash the face;

That thou appear not unto men to fast, but unto the Father which is in secret: thy Father, which seeth, in secret, shall reward thee openly.

Or this brother is going to throw something together.

Aw, I'm so sorry! I promise I will make it up later.

Now my mouth is watery and ready bit down into it. I never know how it is going to taste Paul holding his stomach.

I know you're hungry, me too. I saw two police come in and they were asking questions. And they was showing a picture around.

So, I pretend I'm sick to get you out of there. Before someone see me. I can't afford to get caught before I find Bullet.

Okay, but I wish you would let me grab at least a rib dinner to go.

Hey, we can stop at the next corner to get a bit to eat.

Yes, I know that, but I just want some ribs.

Sorry, we can come back tomorrow when everything has calmed down.

That okay, it's been a long day anyway. And I need a long shower. Maybe I can relax. I hope mom doesn't think I'm coming to church tonight. I'm going to be like you.

What do you mean?

Play sick!

Boy, you better hope God don't crack the sky tonight.

Why?

Because you just told a lie. And you already know where you're going.

Yes, since you said that I guess we both be going together then.

Oh, you got me. I just lied.

Bingo!

Well, in that case Lord please don't come right now.

I got in a hurry up repent before I ended up with a one-way ticket to hell. I know I can't do it, say it in the bible it hot down there. I don't want to take that chance.

But the fearful, and unbelieving, and the abominable, and whoremongers, and sorcerers, and idolaters, and all liars, shall have their part in the lake which burneth wife fire and brimstone: which is the second death.

Okay, I'm coming as we walked toward the bus stop. We saw one of Bullet old friend, he used to hang out together Jeff.

Hey there Jeff! I yelled out and ran up to give him a big hug.

Oh wow, where you have been hiding at. I have seen you in years.

What have you been doing for yourself?

I have been around just working. Hey, meet my friend Paul, we work together. I guess you can say this is my big bear who look out for me.

How have you seen Bullet lately?

Yes, matter of fact I saw him last Thursday night. He stopped by my house for a little while. And he was driving a beautiful car. I think it is black and red.

Are Bullet working now or did he hit a jackpot or something?

Now, this is a good question, I don't know.

Plus, he asked me to go riding with him, but I told him I just got off work. And I was tired and tried to find me something to eat.

I was hungry plus he was drinking. And he knew better because he was still on paper.

If he get put over by the police. He matter well get ready do some time in prison.

A fool hath no delight in understanding, but that his heart may discover itself.

The fear of the LORD is the beginning of knowledge: but fools despise wisdom and instruction.

Wise men lay up knowledge: but the mouth of the foolish in

near destruction.

Because he called me on the same day. He was telling what the judge told him.

That is what made me stop drinking. Now I have a family who is counting on me. I can't let them down. Plus, I'm trying to do the right things.

But I would have you know that the head of every man is Christ; and the head of the woman is the man; and the head of Christ is God.

But is any provide not for his own, and specially for those of his own house, he hath denied the faith, and is worse than an infidel.

You know me, I don't jump into a car with a person driving drunk. That is why one of my brothers is walking with a cane.

Because he jumped into a car with a friend who had been drinking. And he hit a bridge it almost kill him. Now he is in a wheelchair as of today.

But why are you looking for Bullet? Now what did he do?

Think I he stole the car he was driving. They what the police said on the news. And I'm trying to find him before the police catch up with him.

Oh, no I'm glad I didn't get into the car with him now. I could have been in jail for riding in a stealing car.

Now that is mess-up. I thought Bullet had changed his lifestyle for the better.

Now I see he hasn't changed. I hope he isn't still hanging around with the same trouble maker friends.

I had to leave them alone, before someone got hurt or went to prison.

I don't blame you for that. I wish I listened to my friend he tried to tell me the same. I thought I was doing a friend a favor.

But it cost me more trouble than it worth.

I know you heard about the car Bullet was driving on the new someone wrecked it. And they're on the run.

No, I haven't heard that did.

I saw him last Friday night, he asked me to drive him home. Because I was drunk and took Money (friend) home also.

And I did when I was on my way back to his house. So, I was hoping he could be able to drive me home.

But a deer came out in front of me. I tried my best to avoid it, but I lost control of the car.

I ended up hitting a big tree. I was so scared I ran home. Thank God I didn't get hurt. Then the next morning I was getting ready for work. I turned on the television and the news was on.

And the police said they found a car it was stolen.

It was black and red, and they went around asking questions trying to see who was driving the car. That why I need Bullet to clear my name.

Okay, if see him. I will tell you're looking for him. I have got to go now it was good to see you again.

Hey, why did everybody seem like him but all suddenly. We can't find him.

Now, Paul that is a good question. I wish I knew that answer myself. I'm ready to go home too. And you're right it has been a long day too.

That is what I have been wanting to hear all day.

Okay, we can start over tomorrow after work.

Maybe we will have some luck.

Hey, tell your mom I love the lunch that hit the spot.

Yes, I will tell her.

I finally went home. I went straight to my room. Jump in my big chair and take a big breath. I can't wait for this thing to be over. Maybe it all happened for a reason.

I wish I knew what it is. But I learned that some people say they're your friend.

They really isn't most of the time they're trying to get something out of you.

And let us consider one another to provoke unto love and to good works:

Not forsaking the assembling of ourselves together, as the manner of some is; but exhorting one another: and so much the more, as ye see the day approaching.

Or just wanted someone to hang out with them. I'm sorry I didn't listen to Paul he was right.

But I thought I had it all under control. It is trying to control me now; I must fight back to save myself. Lord, I haven't been a good girl lately. Please teach me how to handle all this situation.

"Teach me thy way, O LORD; I will walk in thy truth: unite my heart to fear thy name."

"I will praise thee, O Lord my God with all my heart: and I will glorify thy name for evermore."

"For great is the mercy toward me: and thou hast delivered my soul from the lowest hell."

I better go check in with mom first just to see how day been going. Before I take my shower.

Hey mom, how was your day? Oh, it's okay, did you hear about someone stealing a car and wrecking it.

Yes, ma, I heard about it with my head down.

Why the long look on your face? Something wrong darling?

Na, it has been a long day. I'm okay, I'm going to get into the shower now. And I'm going to put on my night clothes maybe I might watch some television.

Oh, wait a minute, a man came by looking for you today. And I told him you wasn't here. He wanted to know where you were and what time you were back home.

But I didn't tell him anything because he seemed kind of strange. Why will someone come to somebody's house to demand another person's location?

Unless they have some issues (problem) with that person trying to it straight out. Or undercover police looking for someone.

Moreover if thy brother shall trespass against thee, go and tell him his fault between thee and him alone: if he shall hear thee, thou hast gained thy brother.

But if he will not hear thee, then take with thee one or two more, that in the mouth of two or three witness every word may be established.

And if he shall neglect to hear them, tell it unto the church: but if he neglect to hear the church. let him be unto thee as an heathen man and a publican.

Verily I say unto you, Whatsoever ye shall bind on earth shall be bound in heaven: and whatsoever ye shall loose on earth shall be loosed in heaven.

Again I say unto you, That if two of you shall agree on earth as toughing any thing that they shall ask, it shall be done for them of my Father which is in heaven.

For where two or three are gathered together in my name, there am I in the midst of them.

Plus, he looked sacred I didn't open my door I isn't crazy. Are you some type of trouble? Please tell me so me and your father can help you.

No, ma, I'm fine just a little tired today. As I walked back to my room. Thinking maybe that was Bullet who came looking for me. Let's call Paul after I take my shower to let him know what happened.

Hey, Paul, what are you doing?

Oh, nothing just finished dinner and you.

I just finished taking a shower. Mom told me a guy came by here. And asking for me, he was eager to find me. But Mom didn't tell him where I was. I think it was Bullet stop by.

Maybe he probably heard you was looking for him.

If that was so, I wondered why he didn't call me. Instead, come by sacred my mom like that.

Yes, I agree but maybe he lost your number or his phone. This is the only way he could find you.

Yep, maybe you're right. He used to leave his phone at everyone's house. When we go hangout.

That could be a good sign he is still in town. And maybe we can catch up with him. What are you doing tomorrow after work?

Well, nothing so far but I'm still waiting for my rib's dinner.

Okay, we can go by the restaurant and grab plate to go.

Plus, I want to be home before the games starts tonight the first final. And I need to get something from the store also.

For tonight snack on when the game started.

Would you go with me to look for Bullet?

Yes, I go but don't forget I can't stay out long.

Okay, thank you, I will see you in the morning at work.

Don't bring me some breakfast.

I got you. That is the least I can do for your help.

Awa thank you, have good night.

The next morning, I was in the shower and my phone rang. I jumped out of the shower trying to grab the phone. But I fell over the chair and missed the call. When I looked at my phone, I was trying to find who was trying to call me. It was a private number.

Awa, man that could has been Bullet. Or someone who has seen him.

As I put on my shoes it hurtled my feet. Now I can't wear these shoes to work. But I got to wear my sandier.

Hey, good morning Paul! How was your night?

It okay! I'm trying to get ready for work. I wish I could play hooker from work today.

Why?

I just don't feel like go up in there fooling with all these women attitudes. That why I must talk to Jesus every morning to help keep from me going off on some of them.

Yep, I understand. Hey, did you try to call me early.

No, it wasn't me. Why?

Well, someone called me, I was in the shower. But I didn't make it in time. Whoever called it was a private number. So, I couldn't call them back.

Now that was strange I wondered why they didn't leave you a message or something.

Yes, I know.

Hey, have you made it work yet?

No, I'm on my way. I'm still waiting on the bus and you.

No, me too I'm waiting for the bus too. I think I need to save up some money to buy me a car.

Jody darling!

Huh!

I don't think so especially not right now.

Well, maybe you have a good point.

But I'm getting tired trying to catch this dumb bus everywhere go too.

Yep, I do understand, I'm going though it too. Yes, it is

frustrating sometimes especially when you have some things to do. Also, you must wait for others.

Okay, let's me get off this phone the bus coming around this corner.

Paul, I will be there soon.

Okay, I will wait for you outside.

I finally made it work thanks for waiting on me. I bought you three pancakes and some eggs for breakfast. You're going to need it around those ladies today. Mom got up early this morning and made them fresh.

Oh, you tell my mother- in -Law, thanks she just made my day.

You say what?

Oh, I didn't say anything, maybe you heard my belly rumbling.

Na, I heard you right. It sound like you have a crush on me. I smiled huh, I never look at you in that way. Just only a friend.

No, we better let that go. And run a little self-jump in this line to clock in before being late again.

Well, Mr. we have that conservation later.

As we walked into the office every spoke and they were so polite to us.

Paul thank you for the break yesterday. I went home yesterday and cooked for my kids. They didn't give me any trouble.

They even help me around the house. And they went cleanup their room without I'm hollowing and screaming at them.

I used to fuss and fight with them.

You know what God have answer my prayer. Wanda had a big grin on her face.

Please don't thank me just it all to God. As I was taking my seat.

Jody looked at me and gave me a high five.

Let me go to work now.

By that time the boss walked up to me.

Good morning Boss, how are you doing?

Paul, man I feel so good. I told my wife last night. She told me I need to give you and girls a dollar raise starting next week.

You made me realize if you didn't work so hard in this planted.

There be no me thank you for that. He gave me a big hug.

I looked at Jody with a strange look and whispered to her.

I wondered what he had been eating or drinking this morning for breakfast.

Jody burst out laughing.

See, girl don't mess around with God like that. He will hook up.

That Holy Ghost put something on the boss. He had to unload his wallet.

And I will pray the Father, and he shall give you another Comforter, that he may abide with you forever;

Even the Spirit of truth; whom the world cannot receive,

because it seeth him not, neither knoweth him: but ye know him; for he dwelleth with you, and shall be in you.

The bell rang for lunch where we going today?

No, where I get us some pizzas. Jody smiled.

Okay, great I'm hungry too. I will buy sodas.

Hey, Jody, your phone is ranging.

Go ahead and answer it for me. As I was standing in line I get ready warm up the pizzas.

Hello, who speak is this Jody phone?

Yes, this is her phone I may take a message. She is kind of busy at this moment. I will tell her to call you back.

Okay, tell her that Bullet is looking for her.

Hey, wait a minute, I will give her the phone.

Jody came get this phone it is important. I think you might want to answer it.

Hold on, I don't want to get out of this line. Then I will have to go back to the end of line.

Okay then.

Just tell them, I will call them back later.

Okay!

Now who was that calling me? As I walked back to the table.

It was Bullet.

Oh, my God, how could I be that foolish and miss this called. Lord, please let him call back. I grabbed the phone, and I hope I can call him back.

Well, he just called, maybe he will answer this time.

Aw, man he call again from a private number.

It is going to be okay; we're going to find him. So, don't worry.

So that we may boldly say, The Lord is my helper, and I will not fear what man shall do unto me.

Let us therefore come boldly unto the throne of grace, that we may obtain mercy, and find grace to help in time of need.

Wherefor I put thee in remembrance that thou stir up the gift of God, which is in thee by the putting on of my hands.

For God hath not given us the spirit of fear; but of power, and of love, and of a sound mind.

Hey, the news on Joyce yelled out. I wonder what is going on today. As Wanda walked into the breakroom.

If Joyce stop yelling maybe we can all hear it said another co-worker.

It an update on the case last week about the stolen car. Someone came forward to claim the car. He left it with a friend to keep it.

But I told him don't driver it. While I was out of town for a few days.

When I got home on Sunday night the car was missing. I report it was stolen. And the police told me it was a wreck.

If anyone know this guy Bullet Lee Davis where about said the news reporter. Please contact your local police station.

Oh, I'm in big trouble I whisper in Paul ear. I hope Bullet call me back. If I can't get my name clear before Friday. I will do the right thing on Monday and accept my responsibility.

Everything is going to be alright. When we find Bullet and work things out. So, let's go back to work before this bell rings.

I'm to sacred go back to work they might come and get me.

Girl, stop been funny. Just pretend as if nothing happened.

Okay, but that is easier said than done.

Well, yes I know, that when your faith kicks in.

And all things, whatsoever ye shall ask in prayer, believing, ye shall receive.

But without faith it is impossible to please him: for he that cometh to God must believe that he is, and that he is a rewarder of them that diligently seek him.

Now faith is the substance of things hope for, the evidence of things not seen.

So, then faith cometh by hearing, and hearing by the word of God.

For with God nothing shall be impossible.

You got believe something before you go crazy up in here.

Then they're going to think something wrong with you for real.

Paul, why do you make things seem so complicated (difficult).

Na, I'm just trying to help you overcome your fear.

"What time I am afraid, I will trust in thee".

In God I will praise his word, in God I have put my trust; I will not fear what flesh can do unto me.

I sought the LORD, and hear me, and delivered me from all my fears.

Okay!

Well, as the day went on and I was ready to run out of this place. To find Bullet for once for all. I can't keep living like this or I can't sleep. Because I'm afraid the police are going to kick in my door and take me away.

Maybe I could call the television station.

And find out who is the owner of the car. Then go try to be reasoning with him. And let him know that I had no idea that his car had been stolen.

And tell him what really happened. Since I'm suddenly having a hard time finding Bullet.

Let me ask Paul if he would go with me.

If I can get in touch with someone. I pray this will be over soon.

Lord I'm going to make you a promise. I'm going back to church.

And I'm going to give my life back (dedicated) to you. I know this is what you're (God) showing me for years. And had been running from you.

For whom the Lord loveth he chasteneth, and scourgeth every son whom he receiveth.

If ye endure chastening God dealeth with you as with sons:

for what son is he whom the father chasteneth not?

But if ye be without chastisement, wherefore of all are partakers, then are ye bastards, and not sons.

Furthermore we have had father of our flesh corrected us, and gave them reverence: shall we not much rather be in subjection unto the Father of spirits, and live?

For they verily for a few days chastened us after their own pleasure; but he for our profit, that we might be partakers of his holiness.

See, I thought I could do whatever I wanted to do. But allow temptation got the best of me. Yes, I started drinking, smokey marijuana, partying and hanging around the wrong crowd.

I thought if I do people will accept me.

But I see it got me into trouble. Maybe I can't get out of this one. I know everything happen for reasoning and this was the only way you could get attention Lord.

And we know that all things work together for good to them that love God, to them who are the called according to his purpose.

For whom he did foreknow, he also did predestinate to be conformed to the image of his Son, that be that firstborn among many brethren.

Moreover who he did predestinate, them he also called: and whom he called, them he also justified: and whom he justified, them he also glorified.

What shall we then say to these things? If God be for us, who can be against us?

He that spared not his own Son, but delivered him up for us all, how shall he not with him also freely give us all things?

I promise I will make things right if I have to service time. Because I did the crime and tired running.

By that time my phone rang it was Jane.

Hey, I have good news, Bullet called me last night. And said he is turning his in to the police today. But he told me he didn't steal that car.

What do you mean? Jane

He said Lewis's sister gave him the keys and asked him to take her and her friends to the game. He said he asked her did she called her brother to give me permission to drive hir car. And she said yes.

He said he was starting to feel like something wasn't right.

Instead, he called Lewis to ask him for himself. But he believed her.

Ask, and it shall be given you; seek, and ye shall find; knock, and it shall be opened unto you:

For every one that asketh recieveth; and he that seeketh findeth; and to him that knocketh it shall be opened.

But seek ye first the Kingdom of God, and his righteousness; and all these things shall be added unto you.

Maybe all this probably wouldn't be happening. Because he knew she lied to their mother before. About a boy who wanted to see.

And he said one Saturday night he was hanging out at Lewis' house. His little sister called and cried to him (Lewis) because she got dropped off by some friends at a boy's house.

Thinking he liked him because he always flirted with her in front of her friends. But when she knocked on his door it was another over the girl was there. And she didn't have a ride back home.

So, he had to go get her. She told their mother she was going to hang out at some of girlfriend's house. But later she found out the same boy was laughing and joking with his friends that he just wanted to sleep with him.

Lie not one to another, seeing that ye have put off the old man with his deeds;

And have put on the new man, which is renewed in

knowledge after the image of him that created him:

He that worketh deceit shall not dwell within my house: he that telleth lies shall not tarry in my sight.

For nothing is secret, that shall not be made manifest; neither and thing hid, that shall not be known and come abroad.

But those things which proceed out of the mouth come forth from the heart; and they defile the man.

A false witness shall not be unpunished, and he that speaketh lies shall not escape.

He said I didn't know if she was lying to him or not. So, he said he would take them even though he had been drinking early in the day. That is why he asked you to drive the back home. And he wasn't in any shape to drive home. He told me to tell you he was sorry for all this mess (trouble).

The only thing he can do to clear our name was to find Lewis's sister.

And get her to tell her brother that she lied on him. Because she wanted to go to the game to hang out with her friend. Let us pray he drop the charges. So, you guys will be free, but we have a problem he didn't tell me the girl's name. Or Lewis's address.

Aw, man I never knew Lewis. Now this is like looking for a needle in the hay stack.

Yeap!

While a minute they did say his name on the news.

hey Jody!

Huh!

Hold on Jane for a second.

Hey, Paul, did they say on the news who filed the report.

No, they didn't say Lewis's name on the news. But I said Bullet name only.

Hey, who are you talking to?

Jane!

Oh, wow!

He said they didn't mention who filed the police report.

Hey, I will try to call Bullet back and ask him. What is the girl's name and her address. We will be making a home visit today after work.

Okay!

Thanks, maybe we can talk some since in her. Go tell her brother the truth.

Yeap, me too!

Just call me back. Thanks.

Hey, Paul, Jane said Bullet called her last night. And he was trying to get in touch with me.

He wanted to apologize to me. She said he didn't steal the car.
And I heard a loud voice saying in heaven,

Now is come salvation, and strength, and the kingdom of our God, and the power of his Christ: for the accuser of our brethren is cast down, which accused them before our God day and night.

Judge not, according to the appearance, but judge righteous judgment.

But why doth thou judge thy brother? Or why dost thou set at nought thy brother? For we shall all stand before the judgment seat Christ.

For it is written, as live, saith the Lord, every knee shall bow to me, and every tongue shall confess to God.

So then every one of us shall give account of himself to God.

Let us not therefore judge one another anymore: but judge this rather, that no man put a stumbling block or an occasion to fall in his brother's way.

No weapon that is formed against thee shall prosper; and every tongue that shall rise against thee in judgment thou shalt condemn. This is the heritage of the servants of the LORD, and their righteousness is of me, saith the LORD.

She explained to me what really happened. He admit he has been drinking off and on that day.

Plus, he was babysitting at his friend's house for the weekend. While he took his girlfriend to see her mother. And his baby sister came over asking him to drop off her and friends to the game. At first he said no because he didn't have a car.

So, she went into Lewis room and fought his car key.

And he told her brother don't like anyone driving his car. Unless he give them permission.

So, she went outside with the phone in her hand. And he said he was still lying on the couch.

Then she came back into the house and Lewis gave him permission to drive his car. To take her and her friends to the game so he did. In other word she lie on her brother's.

Oh wow, that was so wrong. I bet she don't know how much damage she cause by lying.

You're right about that. I hope she will do the right thing by being honest with her brother. After we confronted her about it.

The lip of truth shall be established for ever: but a lying tongue is but for a moment.

A false witness shall not be unpunished, and he that speaketh lies shall not escape.

Hey, this Jane, I will call you back. I hope she have some good news.

Okay, I got back to work anyway.

I will tell you later.

Hey, Jody, I have been trying to call Bullet. But he isn't answering his phone.

Okay, thanks for trying. When I get off work I'm going to look for the girl. Maybe I will go by the school see to if someone may know her name.

Now that may work, but it don't make sense.

What do you mean? Paul

You don't have her first or her last name.

Well, that is a good point.

My Lord, my Lord what shall I do now?

Hey Paul, do you have something to do after work?

Yes, mom invited me to come with her to church tonight. They're having a revival all week. So, I promised her I will go with her.

Hey, you should come with us. And I will go with you tomorrow after work.

Well, I know I need to go maybe I hear a word. Help me get my life back on track.

Okay, I go with you. What time does it start? Now I don't have any plans tonight.

Oh, it start 7pm.

I be there!

The bell rang to go home as we walked out the door.

My phone rang I was wondering who was calling me.

Hello, who is this?

Selma's daughter Jane.

Okay, now I remember you.

Hey, my uncle Bullet stopped by the house early today. Looking for something to eat. He said mom and you was trying to call him.

He said sorry he missed the call he was sleeping. He gave me this number to give you. 914- 231- 3465. He told me to tell you to call him.

Okay, thanks for calling me.

Why are you smiling Jody?

Oh, that Selma Jane's daughter. She was telling me Bullet stop by their house. Jane wasn't home from work yet. And he said to call him.

Now I have his number.

So, I'm going to call him right now. Ask him do he know Lewis's sister's name. Maybe we can get her to tell the truth about the car. And we are off the hook (free).

And ye shall know the truth, shall make you free.

Hello Bullet, this is Jody.

How have you been doing? And you has been hard to find.

Oh, I'm fine, sorry I have been avoiding your calls. I thought you were the detective. I isn't trying to go back to jail. For something I really didn't do because his sister lied to me. Yes, I know I isn't trying too either.

Hey, I have a plan to clear our names.

Okay, I ran out of ideas, I'm tried running and hiding.

I has been jumping in my sleep scared they're going to kick in my door.

I want to be free again. I made myself a promise that I'm going to stop drinking, smoking and partying with the boys so much.

Hey, guess what?

Huh!

I'm doing the same thing. We can work on this together. Once we clear our names.

Sure, I need someone to give me uphold my commitment. So, that part of the reasoning I got to keep looking over my shoulder.

A man that hath friends must shew himself friendly: and there is a friend that sticketh closer than a brother.

For if they fall, the one will lift up his fellow: but woe to him that is alone when he falleth; for he hath not another to him up.

Every time I walk out of my house.

And I'm afraid the police will always pick on me all my life.

If I don't stary loving myself no one else will. Yes I had to go through something just to see my life flash before me. But that's okay I need it.

Beloved, I wish above all things that thou mayest prosper and be in health, even as thy soul prospereth.

What? Know ye not that your body is the temple of the Holy Ghost which is in you, which ye have of God, are ye are not your own?

For ye are bought with a price: therefore glorify God in your body, and in your spirit, which are God's.

If any man defile the temple of God, him shall God destroy; for the temple of God is holy, which temple ye are.

Be sober, be vigilant; because your adverse the devil, as a roaring loin, walketh about, seeking whom he may devour.

Casting all your care upon him; for he careth for you.

Whom resist stedfast in the faith, knowing that the same afflictions are accomplish in your brethren that are in the world.

I can do all things through Christ which stengtheneth me.

What I mean God can take my life any giving moment. And I won't be ready besides, I'm tied hurting people who love me.

He that covereth his sin shall not prosper: but whoso confesseth and forsaketh them shall have mercy.

But whosoever shall deny me before men, him will I also deny before my Father which is in heaven.

That if thou shall confess with the mouth the Lord Jesus, and shalt believe in thine heart that God hath raised him from the dead, thou shalt be saved.

For with the heart man believeth unto righteousness; and with the mouth confession is made unto salvation.

For the scripture saith, Whosoever believeth on him shall not be ashamed.

Oh, wow, that's great news. I need the name Lewis baby sister name.

Oh, his sister's name is Clover she go to Bama high school. Why do you need to know?

Because we're going to school to try to find her. So, we can talk to her. Why did she lie to her brother? And I hope we can talk her into she will tell her brother the truth.

Oh, okay that sound a good plan.

I will call you back and let you know what happened.

Thanks!

We finally made it to school. We stood in the parking lot. Waiting for the bell to ring. Hoping she was there.

Kids running everywhere boy how we're going find this girl. Jody.

Hey, we're going to pretend that we're Clover parents. And we're looking for maybe someone who will point her out from this crowds.

That is a good idea we had better be careful. We don't want to get caught by the security guard. Then we were really in big trouble.

Okay, Paul, thanks I know we will for sure be on the news. Accused of kidnap a child.

We started asking around do anyone know a girl named Clover who go to this school. But no one pay us any attend us. We walked half way around the school campus.

No one seemed to know this girl. But a young boy finally walked up to me, and I know Clover because she is in my class. She isn't here because our teacher told us she will be back coming to school tomorrow.

She had been out of school for a week now.

"Can any hide himself in secret places that I shall not see him? saith the LORD.

Do not I fill heaven and earth? Saith the LORD."

"For there is nothing covered, that shall not be revealed; neither hid, that shall not be known."

"Therefore whatsoever ye have spoken in darkness shall be heard in the light; and that which ye have spoken in the ear in closets shall be proclaimed upon the housetops."

"And I say unto you my friends, Be not afraid of them that kill the body, and after that have no more that they can do."

"But I will forewarn you whom ye shall fear: Fear him, which after he hath killed hath power to cast into hell; yea, I say unto you, Fear him."

I hope she isn't in trouble or sick. She was telling another girl. How she felt kind of bad, because she told a little lie to her brother. If he find out he just may kill me.

So, she could be at the game with her friends. Later she found her brother's car had been in a wreck. And now her brother got mad at his friend for driving his car without his permission.

Also, she wanted to see this boy and she got a crush on him. I overheard them talking about it in the hallway the other morning before we started class last week

Oh, thank you. Here you five dollars go buy something with it. But you can't tell anyone you were talking to us.

Okay, yea ma, thanks.

Now, what are we going to do? We don't have much time; I have got to go home and get ready for church. Did you forget?

Okay, Paul let go. I'm going to come back after work tomorrow. I pray this time we find her.

Let me call Bullet back and let him know we didn't have any luck. Because she wasn't there.

Hi, we did find out what school she attended. But she wasn't there because one of her classmates told me she hadn't been to school in a week.

So, we're going back to school hoping this time we will find some luck once for all. Have you ever heard her talking to a friend, she hang out with.

No but she always talks to a girl named Linda on the phone. But I never met her.

What are we going to do now? If we can't find her. I guess we will have to tell Lewis ourselves. What really happened. That is the only thing we can do to be honest.

These six things doth the LORD hate: yea, seven are an abomination unto him:

A proud look, a lying tongue, and hands that shed innocent blood,

Better is the poor that walketh in his integrity, than he that is perverse in his lips, and is a fool.

Finally, brethren, whatsoever things are true, whatsoever things are honest, whatsoever things are just, whatsoever things are pure, whatsoever things are lovely, whatsoever things are of good report; if there be any virtue, and if there be any praise, think on these things.

Those things, which ye have both learned, and received, and heard, and seen in me, do: and the God of peace shall be with you.

And as ye would that men should do to you, do ye also to them likewise.

And I pray he drop the charge on you. Because he didn't know I wrecked the car.

But don't worry I will go with you. And I will help you explain what happened.

Thanks Jody!

I'm truly sorry for putting you in my mess (problem) Jody. That is one of the reasons I must stop doing things that isn't right. I'm hurting many people who love me.

Hey, when I get out of this trouble let us all go to church together. Girl, I got charged myself I had a dream that I was in prison.

How people sell themselves out to survive. And everyday someone hates each other. They will Pay other to kill you that why you must watch your step ever moment of the day. And you're afraid to sleep you thinking someone will rape you.

Half of them have life they will never get out of prison.

Until death so, some don't care what they do.

Because some feel like they don't have anything to look forward to too.

I don't want to live like that. I know God have something better plain for me. I just needed to settle down and asked him to show me my purpose in my life.

Before I formed thee in the belly I knee thee; and before thou camest forth out of the womb I sanctified thee, and I ordained thee a prophet unto the nations.

Then said I, Ah, Lord, GOD, behold, I cannot speak: for I am a child.

But the LORD said unto me, Say not I am a child: for thou shalt go to all that I shall send thee, and whatsoever command thee thou shalt speak.

Be not afraid of their faces: for I am with thee to deliver thee, saith the LORD.

Then the LORD put forth his hand and touched my mouth. And the LORD said unto me, Behold, I have put my words in thy mouth.

See, I have this day set thee over the nations and over the kingdoms, to root out, and to pull down, and destroy, and to throw down, to build, and to plant.

For I know the thoughts that I think toward you, saith the LORD, thoughts of peace, and not of evil, to give you an expected end.

Train up a child in the way he should go: and when he is old, he will not depart from it.

And we know that all things work together for good to them that love God, to them who are the called according to his purpose.

And he said unto me, My grace is sufficient for thee: for my strength in made perfect in weakness. Most gladly therefore will I rather glory in my infirmities, that the power of Christ may rest upon me.

Mom had me and Jane in church every Wednesday and Sunday. Somehow we slowly went to the church. I guess when my mom got sick. And we all pray to God make her better. But she got worse and in that same year she die.

For if our heart condemn us, God is greater than our heart, and knoweth all things.

For whether we live, we live unto the Lord; and whether we die, we die unto the Lord: whether we live therefore, or die, we are the Lord's.

And whosoever liveth and believeth in me shall never die. Believest thou this?

Then shall the dust return to the spirit shall return unto God who gave it.

And fear not them, which kill the body, but are not able to kill the soul: but rather fear him which is able to destroy both soul and body in hell.

And God shall wipe away all tears from their eyes; and there shall be no more death, neither sorrow shall be any more pain: for the former things are passed away.

 After mom I started blame God for let her die. And I alone but our auntie was so sweet to me. And keep us in church. It just wasn't the same because mom isn't there.

When I got older I stayed away from church.

For if we sin wilfully after that we have received the knowledge of the truth, there remaineth no more sacrifice for sins,

There is a way which seemeth right unto a man, but the end thereof are the ways of death.

For if after they have escaped the pollutions of the world through the knowledge of the Lord and Saviour Jesus Christ, they are again entangled therein, and overcome, that latter end is worse with them than the beginning.

For it is happened unto them according to the true proverb, The dog is turned to his own vomit again; and the sow that was washed to her wallowing in the mire.

Say unto them, As I live, saith the Lord GOD, I have no pleasure in the death of the wicked; but that the wicked turn from his way and live: ye, turn ye from your evil ways; for why will ye die, O house of Isreal?

I started drinking, smoking and hanging around with people who didn't mean me any good. Trying to run from the pain.

Every time I used to visit my aunt Bunny she always reminded me of what mom used to tell me.

Son I love you, but God love you more. And please always put him first in your life and he guide you.

For God so loved the world, that he gave his only begotten Son, that whosoever believeth in him should not perish, but have everlasting life.

For God sent not his Son into the world to condemn the world; but that the world through him might be saved.

I will instruct thee and teach thee in the way which thou shalt go: I will guide thee with mine eye.

He will show you things and take you places that I couldn't.

Since you're older please look out for your little sister. But when I started getting into trouble Jane always bailed me out. I feel so bad I let her down so many times. When I made a promise to mom and my auntie.

That I would take care of her. If mom could see me know she would be so disappointed with me. I have a little boy I haven't seen in years.

What? You never told you about having a child. Jody with a surprised look on her face.

No, because at first I was ashamed of it. I was young and it slipped up I made a baby. I was so scared I ran from my responsibility.

For every man shall bear his own burden.

But if any provide not for his own, and specially for those of his own house, he hath denied the faith, and is worse than an infidel.

And that servant, which knew his lord's will and prepared not himself, neither did according to his will, shall be beaten with many stripes.

But he that knew not, and did commit things worthy of stripes, shall be beaten with stripes. For into whomsoever much is given, of him shall be much required: and whom men have committed much, of him they will ask the more.

Okay!

Now it is time for me to step up and do the right thing. If his mother give me a chance.

If not I understand because of my decision I chose.

Even though my father wasn't around me.

The last time I saw dad at my mom's funeral was eight years ago. And he sat at the back of the church. He didn't speak to us. I started to grow bitter toward him.

I think I started acting like him toward my son.

For I know him, that he will command his children and his household after him, and they shall keep the way of the LORD, to do justice and judgment; that the LORD may bring upon Abraham that which he hath spoken of him.

Hear, ye children, the instruction of a father, and attend to know understanding.

For I give you good doctrine, forsake ye not my law.

For I was my father's son, tender and only beloved in the sight of my mother.

He taught me also, and said unto me, Let thine heart retain my words: keep my commandments, and live.

Get wisdom, get understanding: forget it not; neither decline from the words of my mouth.

Forsake her not, and she shall preserve thee: love her, and she shall keep thee.

Wisdom is the principal thing; therefore get wisdom: and with all thy getting get understanding.

Exalt her, and she shall promote thee: she shall bring thee to honour, when thou dost embrace her.

She shall give to thine head an ornament of grace: a crown of glory shall deliver to thee.

A good man leaveth an inheritance to his children's children: and the wealth of the sinner is laid up for the just.

I have no greater joy than to hear that my children walk in truth.

I spend more time in the street than with him. I pray he will allow me to be in his life.

I don't want to be like father, he wasn't around and regret it for the rest of my life.

Especially for holidays and birthdays. But I already miss a few of them. I can't afford to miss anymore.

I bet my father don't know when my birthday is anymore. I never received a gift or any from him that I can remember. Tears ran down my face.

Oh, wow Bullet, you never know what a person is going though or been though. I'm sorry but you need to tell these other guys your stories.

Because you aren't the only one who had too though this.

I know it would help others get on the right path. Jody had tears in her eyes.

And they overcame him by the blood of the Lamb, and by the word of their testimony; and they loved not their lives unto the death.

Therefore rejoice, ye heavens, and ye that dwell in them. Woe to the inhabiters of the earth and of the sea! For the devil is come down unto you, having great wrath, because he that he hath but a short time.

I don't know why people want to hear my sad story.

Yes, someone will be listening, I did.

Okay, first let us get out of this problem. I promise I will share my story.

Hey, Bullet, I got to go home and get ready for church. I promised Paul I would go with him.

I knew something different about him.

Yea, me too. I'm thankful to be a great friend to me. I will call you tomorrow when I get off work. I guess I will go back to the school to see if Linda is still going there. Since we can't find Clover.

Okay! Please pray for me while you're there.

Paul let go home I don't want us to be late for church.

Yes, I know! I don't want my mother to be looking up side my head with that mean look. Because I'm late trying stay on her good side.

Hey, I will meet you at the church tonight. It start at 7.

Oh, what is the name of the New Zion church on the corner of 37th. It is over by the clothing shop.

Okay, I know where it is.

I finally made it home.

Hey mom, how are you doing?

I'm okay but why is this big kiss coming from Miss. Jody. As she is getting ready to start her dinner. Are you okay?

Yea, ma! Oh, my friend Paul asked me if I would like to go to a revival with him. And I told him I would.

Oh, really! What made you want to go? Or did you trip up on something and hit your head.

No ma! Wow, me and your father has been begging for years to come back to church. It take a man huh.

Na, mom isn't like that I wasn't ready, sometime a situation make you realize you need God. He don't need us. But he still accept us to be his children.

If ye abide in me, and my words abide in you, ye shall ask what ye will be done unto you.

''But whosoever shall deny me before men, him will I also deny before my Father which is in heaven.''

First I got to find something to put on. It have been a long time since I set foot in a church.

Yep, that's true you better take a water hose with you.

Mom! Why? As I walk toward my room.

The church might catch on fire because you enter the building. You had better look around to see where all the exits are. You just might have to break for a door. Or you may be run over.

See, mom that isn't funny.

Oh, who is laughing? Well, I'm just telling you the truth.

Maybe this may be me starting back going more often. Okay now I get ready before I be late fooling around you mom.

Aw, I haven't had any fun with you in a while.

Because you're always gone or at work. We need a mommy and a daughter day out.

Okay, mom sorry can we talk about it later? Right now, I have something going on I promise. Soon I will take care of a few things. I will take you out anywhere you want to go. But if any widow have children or nephews, let them learn first to shew piety at home, and to requite their parents: for that is good and acceptable before God.

Alright, now I better write that on the calendar. So, I won't forget this? Hey, make sure you pray for me and your old daddy while you're there.

Well, okay baby.

Hey Paul, I'm on my way. Where are you at?

Oh, I'm almost ready I be their shorty. And I'm riding with the (Queen) mom.

Okay, I be out front waiting for you. I don't want to go in the church alone.

Hey Jody, this is my famous mother Janet. This is my friend and co-worker.

It is good to finally meet you, Paul talk about you all the time at work. I just love your cooking.

Huh!

One day Paul shared his lunch with me.

Okay, thanks I got to invite you one Sunday for dinner after church.

Paul looked over at Jody and waited on her response.

Oh, I would love to come maybe you can talk about Paul's baby stories. And show me his baby picture.

Girl, yes, I got a lot of them. Paul I'm beginning to like her already.

Hold up mom, do I have a say do this? I look up at her.

No!

Wow, that is not fair, you girls gang up on me.

Boy, I'm your mom you always remember that. But I love

you she smiled.

Mom, we will talk about this later. We had better go in before the start. And it will be hard to find good seating.

I looked around at people standing all over the hall. The Deacon was tall and slim. Please stand for the prayer.

Lord, I (Jody) know I can use some of that right. I close my eyes and pray this mess will be over soon. Then he told us please take our seats.

After this manner therefore pray ye: Our Father which art in heaven, Hallowed be thy name.

Thy kingdom come. Thy will be done in earth, as it is in heaven.

Give us this day our daily bread.

And forgive us our debts as we forgive our debtors.

And Lead us not into temptation, but deliver us from evil: For thine is the kingdom, and the power, and the glory, forever.

Amen.

I whisper over to Paul; man, this church is too big for me. I will get lost in here if I was trying to find the bathroom. Paul smiled.

The preacher stood up and said I hope everyone bought their sword (bible) with them. If not you can follow on the big screen.

Hey, Mrs. Janet, what do he mean?

Oh, child he is talking about your bible.

I was so embarrassed; it reminded me that I haven't been to a church so long or read my bible. Now I'm starting to feel bad, knowing how God keep his eyes on me. Keep me from harm and damage.

And the Lord shall deliver me from every evil work, and will preserve me unto his heavenly kingdom: to whom be glory for ever and ever.

No weapon that is formed against thee shall prosper; and every tongue that shall rise against thee in judgment thou shalt condemn.

This is the heritage of the servants of righteousness is of me saith the LORD.

Though I walk in the midst of trouble, thou wilt revive me: thou shalt stretch froth thine hand against the wrath of mine enemies, and thy right hand shall save me.

All is shall come to pass, if thou shalt hearken diligently unto the voice of the LORD thy God, to observe and to do all his commandment which I command thee this day, that the LORD thy God will set thee on high above all nations of the earth:

And all these blessings shall come on thee, and overtake thee, if thou shalt hearken unto the voice of the LORD the God. The God of my rock; in him will I trust: he is my shield, and the horn of my salvation, my high tower, and my refuge, my saviour; thou savest me from violence.

I will call on the LORD, who is worthy to be praised: so shall I be saved from mine enemies.

All my life a tear dropped from my eyes.

Knowing I need to repent and ask God to forgive me. This I know mom and dad keep us in church.

Here I'm ten years later because my life has turned upside down. Thought ran my mind as I sat there.

Submit yourselves therefore to God.

Resist the devil, and he will flee from you.

Oh, wow I ran out the house and forget my bible. I guess I haven't picked it in a while. That Problem why I forget.

Well, you can share my bible with me. Mrs. Janet smiled as she slid over.

Okay thanks.

Please open it to Mattew 6:33 king James version and stand for the reading:

But seek ye first the kingdom of God, and his righteousness; and all these things shall be added unto you.

You may be seated.

Let me start with this old saying, if you don't put God in everything you do. See a lot of you wondering why God haven't honor your prayer. I stopped by for a few minutes. And tell you a little secret. But it isn't really a secret. But God don't hide anything from us.

It is because some of you don't go search for it. Meaning don't get into his words. By reading the Lord word.

My people are destroyed for lack of knowledge: because thou

hast rejected knowledge,

I will also reject thee, that thou be no priest to me: seeing thou hast forgotten the law of the God, I will also forget the children.

Comforter, which is the Holy Ghost, whom the Father will send in my name, he shall teach you all things, and bring all things to your remembrance, whatsoever I have said unto you.

And rather not read it because once you know the word you're required to be obedient to his word.

For it had been better for them not to have known the way of righteousness, than, after they have known it, to turn from the holy commandment delivered unto them.

Who will have all men to be saved, and to come unto the knowledge of the truth.

For there is one God, and one mediator between God and men, the man Christ Jesus:

And they shall teach no more every man his neighbour, and every man his brother, saying, Know the LORD: for they shall all know me, from the least of them unto the greatest of them, saith the LORD: for I will forgive their iniquity, and I will remember their sin no more.

Whosoever therefore shall break one of these least commandments and shall teach men so, he shall be called the least in the kingdom of heaven: but whosoever shall do and teach them, the same shall be called great in the kingdom of heaven.

But you can't fall asleep on me. You miss it because some of us say they love the Lord. You won't put him first in your life. And we want to keep doing whatever, think God going to rewarded you for that.

But seek ye first the kingdom of God, and his righteousness;

and all these things shall be added unto you.

Seek ye the LORD while he may be found, call ye upon him while he is near:

Let the wicked forsake his way, and the unrighteous man his thoughts: and let him return unto the LORD, and he will have mercy upon him; and to our God, for he will abundantly pardon.

For my thought are not your thoughts, neither are your ways my ways saith the LORD.

"For as the heavens are higher than the earth, so are my ways higher than your ways, and my thoughts than your thoughts."

Oh, if you didn't know yes you will receive a reward, but you just may not like it. Let me explain I see some have a surprise look on some of your face.

And behold, I come quickly; and my reward is with me, to give evert man according as his work shall be.

I the LORD search the heart, I try the reins, even to give every man according to his ways, and according to the fruit of his doings.

Knowing that whatever good thing ant man doeth, the same he receive of the Lord, whether he be bond or free.

Delight thyself also in the LORD; and he shall give thee the desires of thine heart.

Oh, another thing God isn't a toy you can play with him anytime. And when you get tired of playing with him you can put him in a box. But when you need him you can pull him back out of the box any time.

There are six things the LORD hates seven that are detestable to him: haughty eyes, a lying tongue, hands that shed innocent blood, a heart that devises wick schemes, feet that are quick to rush into evil, a false witness who pours out lies and a man who stirs up descension among brothers.

He hate when we put him on the back seat.

Instead, we allow him to be the first in your life.

For you shall worship no other god. For the Lord, whose name is Jealous, is a jealous God.

God is jealous, and the LORD revengeth; the LORD revengeth, and is furious; the LORD will take vengeance on his adversaries, and he reserveth wrath for his enemies.

Neither their silver nor gold shall be able to deliver them in the day of the LORD'S wrath;

but the whole land shall be devoured by the fire of his jealousy: for he shall make even a speedy riddance of all them that dwell in the Land.

Therefore wait ye upon me, saith the LORD, until the day that I rise up to the prey: for my determination is to gather the nations, that I may assemble the kingdoms, to pour upon them mine indignation, even all my fierce anger: for all the earth shall be devoured with the fire of my jealousy.

That may ye the children your Father which is in heaven: for he maketh his sun to rise on the evil and on good, and sendeth rain on the just and unjust.

For if ye love them which love you, what reward have ye? Do not even the publicans the same?

And if ye salute your brethren only,

what do ye more than others? Do not even the publicans so?

"Be ye therefore perfect, even as your Father which is in heaven is Perfect."

If you won't let him into your life.

I call heaven and earth to record this day against you, that I have set before you life and death, blessing and cursing: therefore choose life, that both thou and thy seed may live:

That thou mayest love the LORD thy God, and that thou mayest obey his voice, and that thou mayest cleave unto him: for he is thy life, and the length of thy days: that the thou mayest dwell in the land which the LORD sware unto thy father, to Abraham, to Isaac, and to Jacob, to give them.

That is your choice. Let us look at Psalm 37:3-5 in the King James Version bible. I'm using.

So, we can go home maybe I can grab a piece of chicken leg. Someone calling my name it is saying Pastor please my feed.

''Wow be unto the pastors that destroy and scatter the sheep of my pasture! Saith the LORD.''

Therefore thus saith LORD God of Isreal against the pastors that feed my people; Ye have scattered my flock, and driven them away, and have not visited them: behold, I will visit upon you the evil of your doings, saith the LORD.

And I will gather the remnant of my flock out of all countries whither I have driven them, and will bring to their folds; and they shall be fruitful and increase.

 And I will set up shepherds over them which shall feed them: and they shall fear no more, nor be dismayed, neither shall they be lacking, saith the LORD.

They all burst out laughing.

But he isn't the only hungry Paul whispered over me (Jody).

Boy, when you're never hungry? I bet you have been dreaming about food in your sleep.

Girl, how do you know that?

Mom looked up at them just shaking her head.

Trust I the Lord, and do good; so shalt thou dwell in the land, and verily thou be fed.

Delight thyself also in the Lord; and he shall give thee the desires of thine heart.

Commit the way unto the Lord; trust also in him; and he shall bring it to pass.

Now that is the secret someone mark this down. Trust in the Lord that his promise to us all who chose him.

Oh, I almost forgot this one too.

I have been young and now am old; yet have I not seen the righteous forsaken, nor seed begging bread.

Let us stand to be dismissed.

Oh, that is the type of message make you wondered what God up too. Paul thank you for inviting me. That preacher was talking to me. I need to hear that don't give up on him.

No matter what you're facing in your life.

For God hath not given us the spirit of fear; but of power,

and of love, and of a sound mind.

Be not thou therefore ashamed of the testimony of our Lord, nor of me his prisoner: but be thou

partaker of the afflictions of the gospel according to the power of God;

who have saved us, and called us with an holy calling, not according to our works, but according to his own purpose and grace, which was given us in Christ Jesus before the world began,"

But is now made manifest by the appearing of our Saviour Jesus Christ, who hath abolished death, and hath brought life and immortality to light through the gospel:

Whereunto I am appointed a preacher, and an apostle, and a teacher of the Gentiles.

For the which cause I also suffer these things: nevertheless I am not ashamed: for I know whom I have believed, and am persuaded that he is able to keep that which I have committed unto him against that day.

Hold fast the form of sound words, which thou hast heard of me, in faith and love which is in Christ Jesus.

I know I'm going home to repent and look back over my life. And ask God please work on me. And I don't won't keep living my life this way anymore.

I can do all things through Christ which strengtheneth me.

Be ye strong therefore, and let not your hands be weak: for your work shall be rewarded.

For I know the thought that I think toward you, saith the LORD, thought of peace, and not of evil, to give you an expected end.

And we know that all things work together for good of them that love God, to them who are the called according to his purpose.

Oh! The Spirit of God got you. Huh.

Yeap, something like that. I smiled as we got ready to leave the church.

I heard a voice.

Mrs. Mrs.

I looked around the room.

Jody the Pastor want to talk to you.

Are you sure? Paul

Yes! I looked it up at her.

Why?

I don't know! I'm not a psychic (minded reader).

Sorry, but didn't want to disturb you. But the Holy Spirit won't let go home. Until I ask you I can play for you.

Yes, sir I need it. I smiled.

The Pastor begin to pray for me. I felt something falling on me.

Before I knew it I was shouting (dancing) all round the church. Tears was pouring all down my face. I just praising God, I didn't care who saw me.

Hey, mom, look at her, she is getting her break though I whisper.

Yep, this is like our God giving us what we need at right timing.

But they that LORD shall renew their strength; they shall mount up with wings as eagles; they shall run, and not be weary; and they shall walk, and not faint.

Because to every purpose there is time and Judgment, therefore the misery of man is great upon him.

But, beloved, be not ignorant of this one thing, that one day is with the Lord as thousand years, and a thousand years as one day.

For the vision is yet for an appointed time, but at the end it shall speak, and not lie: though it tarry, wait for it;

because it will surely come, it will not tarry.

To every thing there is a season, and a time to every purpose under the heaven:

Hey, I see you got your breakthrough. Paul smiled.

Yes I did, and now I feel so refreshed. Well, thanks again for inviting me. I will see you in the morning. As she walked around to the bus stop.

Okay, I got to get home myself. I'll call you soon, I got home Paul.

Good morning, Paul &Jody, you two look refreshed. You two must get some good night's rest. As Wanda comes into the breakroom.

Yes I did, but you missed a powerful message last night.

What do you mean?

Oh, Paul invited me to his mother's church. They're having a revival. And the Lord showered his spirit down on me.

Girl, I feel like a brand-new person.

Aw, man I should've been there too. Maybe I could've got these demons (evil spirit) out of my kids.

And unclean spirits, when they him, fell down before him, and cried, saying, Thou art the Son of God.

Thou believest that there is one God; thou doest well: the devils also believe, and tremble.

Be sober, be vigilant; because your adversary the devil, as a roaring lion, walketh about, seeking whom he may devour: Put on the whole armour of God, that ye may be able to stand against the wiles of the devil.

For we wrestle not against flesh and blood, but against principalities, against powers, against the rulers of the darkness of this world, against spiritual wickedness in high places.

Submit yourselves therefore to God. Resist the devil, and he will flee from you.

And the angels which kept not their first estate, but left their own habitation, he hath reserved in everlasting chains under darkness unto the judgment of the great day.

Paul looked at me with a funny look on his face. I tried my best better not to burst out laughing at her. But I couldn't help myself.

Oh, Sorry!

It okay! Because that is the truth.

Oh yes, that mean you're going to get some work out today.

I see you have joked this morning.

Yep, she walked out of the breakroom heading to the office.

Okay, I can't wait to get this thing over with. Paul whispered under his breath.

Well, me too. Let's go get this day over maybe we will have some luck finding Lewis's sister after work.

I know that right.

Hey, I meet you in the office, I better stop by this bathroom. Before I look up in these women crazy faces.

Okay!

Hey, ladies and gentlemen it been post we got to work over this week.

The boss left a memo saying we have a new contract. And we got to start working on it.

Wanda shouted out.

Aw, man, that mean the school will be closed.

Yeap!

When we get off work all this week. Now what I'm going to do? Paul you have your wish; you're getting some over time.

Aw, no I don't! That mean I will be missing my games. You know I love my basketball. I used to play in school.

Oh, I didn't know that.

My phone rang I looked down it was Jane.

Paul, I had better answer this.

Okay!
I ran to the bathroom to see if she had got some good news.

Hello Jody, they found Bullet as she was crying.

What do this mean?

The police arrested him and took him to jail. And this was his third strike. So isn't looking for him.

I don't know yet, but we better hurry up and get this mess (problem) straight out. Before he stood before the judge. And pray that the judge let him go. Or he will be going to prisoner.

What can we do to help him to get out of this trouble.

Right now, first we need to find that girl. Who lied to him and prayed she will tell the truth. Maybe the judge will have some mercy on him.

Oh, okay!

I'm going to go see him today. After I got off work. I will call you back with the details.

Okay, thanks, Jane for letting me know.

I walked out of the bathroom with tears in my eyes.

Hey, Jody, what's wrong with you? I (Paul) looked up and ran over to her.

She told me the police finally arrested Bullet.

Aw, no he's just trying to get his life back on track. What are we going to do now?

Let not your heart be troubled: ye believe in God also in me.

A woman when she is in travail hath sorrow, because her hours is come: but as soon as she is delivered of the she remembereth no more the anguish, for joy that a man is born into the world.

And ye now therefore have sorrow: but I will see you again, and your heart shall rejoice, and your joy no man taketh from you.

And in that day ye shall ask me nothing. Verily, verily, I say unto you, Whatsoever ye shall ask the Father in my name, he will give it you.

Hitherto have ye asked nothing in my name: ask, and ye shall receive, that your joy may be full."

"These things have I spoken unto you in proverbs: but the time coneth, when I shall no more speak unto you in proverbs, but I shall shew you plainly of the Father.

At that day ye shall ask in my name: and I say not unto you, that I will pray the Father for you:

For the Father himself loveth you, because ye have loved me, and have believed that I came out from God.

These things I have spoken unto you, that in me ye might have peace. In the world ye shall have tribulation: but be of good cheer;

I have overcome the world.

 I don't know yet! But we needed to hurry up and find Lewis's sister.

Jane said she is going to see him after she get off work later.

And she said she will call me later.

Yep, if we can find Lewis maybe we can reason with him. After we tell him Bullet side of his story. Bullet told us it was his sister who lied to him. This isn't right let an innocent man go to prison for something he didn't do.

Yep, I agree with you. I hope he will believe us.

Hey, we better go back to work. Before we get into trouble.

Okay, it's going to be alright.

Before we knew it was lunch time.

My phone was off it, I didn't know I accidentally turned off my phone.

Hey, Jody why are your phone vibrator? Oh, maybe someone have sent me a message.

I check it when I get into the breakroom.

Hey Jody!

Huh!

Come here please.

Okay, first let me warm our food up. If I get out of this line lunch will be half way over.

Oh okay! As I sat down and grabbed her phone checking my text, it was a message from Selma (Jane's daughter).

My mom told me you was looking for a girl named Clover who go to the same school I attended. I know her, she is in one of my classes.

I will help you guys to tell you that not right she lie on my uncle.

Just because she wanted to go to a game. I will confront her and probably beat her up.

The LORD shall fight for you, and ye shall hold your peace.

Oh, I better text her back and pled to her not get herself into a fight with her.

The bell rang to go home.

Hey, we need to go to Jane house later. So, we can put a plan together. Maybe I can get Selma to invite Clover to her house. Then she work on her mind, and she have no choice but to tell the truth. And we're going to record her also.

So, we can have some evidence to prove to Lewis it was his sister who caused all this head-ack.

It has been going on for a long time making everyone miserable. I bet if someone lied to her, she wouldn't like it. Or she would be ready to fight.

And as ye would that men should do to you, do ye also to them likewise.

And be ye kind one to another, tenderhearted, forgiving me another, even as God for Christ's sake hath forgiven you.

Finally, be ye all of one mind, having compassion one of another, love as brethren, be pitiful, be courteous:

Not rendering evil for evil, or railing for railing: but contrariwise blessing; know that ye are thereunto called, that ye should inherit a blessing.

For he that will love life, and see good days, let him refrain his tongue from evil, and his lips that they speak no guile.

Let him eschew evil, and do good; let him seek peace, and ensue it.

We don't need her to be in trouble too.

Hey, what's going on now? Paul sat down.

I'm going to text her back to let her know isn't worth it. Please don't do that, your uncle don't want to see you in trouble over him.

We're going to tell her brother what she has done. And let him deal with her.

He that spareth his rod hateth his son: but he that loveth him chasteneth him betimes.

Yes you're right, that won't solve the problem. But it will cause more.

That is true.

The phone rang it was Jane.

Hello!

This is Jane, I visited Bullet today. And he said he will be going to court next month. Because he broke his probation. They is talking about giving him five years in prison.

If we can prove it to the judge. That Bullet didn't steal the car it was all a lie. They don't have any choice but to drop the charges on him. And pray they let go free.

Okay, we will go to Lewis ourselves and let him know what happened sister lie to him.

Oh, Jane!

Huh!

Selma, text me early saying Lewis's sister is in one of the classes. So, what me and Paul came up with ask Selma invite to your house. We will make her confess what she has done.

Plus, we will be recording her so have some evidence. She won't be able to lie her way out of this one.

Yes, let's do that.

The bell rang the kids running all over the place. We will never find her in this crowd.

Jody, let us back up and let Selma find her for us. We don't want to frighten her.

 She may report us to the school security guard. Then we will be more trouble thinking we're trying to kidnap her.

Well, you're right! I never thought of it that way.

Hey, Clover, come here for a minute. I wanted you to meet

someone.

Okay, it's better to be a boy.

Well, something like that.

Hey, I'm Jody, a young girl and you need to go with us right now. Because you have a lot of explanations to do.

Oh, what are you talking about lady? Clover broke out running through the crowd.

Waiting a minute, she didn't know how she hurt my uncle. Just meet me around the corner away from the school.

I will catch her promise. Miss. Jody.

Okay!

Selma took off and ran behind her.

Hey, Miss. Jody, I told her what she done to my family. Selma was breathing heavily. Here I caught her.

Thanks!

Clover, I'm warning you if you don't tell us the truth. I'm going to give you a black eye. Because you let your brother believe that my uncle Bullet took his car without permission.

You know you told him that you call your brother. And you ask him for permission.

So, Uncle Bullet can drive his car so that he can take you to the game. And you knew he was there to watch over your brother's house.

He said he was drinking that day.

And you took advantage of him. You already know your brother don't like to let others drive their car without his permission.

Now my uncle is about to go to prison. Selma screams at her, tears running down your face. Now how you feel that if done the same to your brother.

Or anyone in your family. I know you wouldn't like it. I told you what if I don't remember what I done. I'm going to remember it. I hope you start playing like you have amnesia (memory loss). As I (Selma) ball up my fist, my face turned red with rage in my eyes. You have five minutes to rethink that question.

As a matter of fact, your mother is going to hear what you

have done. Send an innocent man to prison. Because of your selfishness.

So, you had better think fast or you're going to need an ambulance.

When I mess up your pretty face. Because I'm going to beat you up and lie about it I didn't do it. Since you want to play this dirty game.

Okay, okay I did it. What I must do is make things right. First you can call Lewis and tell meet you down at the police station.

Because you have something to confess.

Confess your faults one to another, and pray one for another, that ye may be healed. The effectual fervent prayer of a righteous man availeth much.

That if thou shalt confess with thy mouth the Lord Jesus, and shalt believe in thine heart that God hath raised him from the dead, thou shalt be saved.

For with the heart man beliveth unto righteousness; and with the mouth confession is made unto salvation.

For the scripture saith, Whosoever believeth on him shall not be ashamed.

For it is written, As I live, saith the Lord, every knee shall bow to me, and every tongue shall confess to God.

So then everyone of us shall give account of himself to God.

Here is my phone so just dial it Jody and Paul said it at the same time.

Okay, I will, hey Lewis, this is Clover I need you to come down at the police station right now.

I hope you isn't in trouble. Because I will be very upset with you. Okay let me throw on some clothes and see what is going on. He yelled.

Girl, what have you done now? I'm on my way just sitting tight. I got to tell mom to let her know you're down at the police station. And you already know she may come too.

Hey, where are you going in a hurry? Boy. And where Clover is supposedly be out of school by now. And on her way home.

Mom, I will go look for her.

She probably stopped by one of her friends' houses for a minute. I will be back soon. Sorry, Lord for lying, I didn't want mom to start stressing out. Until I find out what is going on.

I jumped into the car and ran down to the station. And ran up the stairs And I got half way was out of breath.

Clover, why are you down here?

Well, I sort of lie about your car. When you ask about it.

What do you mean? Lewis yelled at her. And this time you had better tell me the truth. Or I'm going to let you stay down here.

And who are you guys.

Oh, we will tell you who we're when Clover confess to you.

Okay! He looked at us with a strange look on his face.

Okay, I will tell you with tears in her eyes. I lied to you when you were out of town. And I knew Bullet were babysitting your house for the weekend for you.

I told him that I got permission from you so that he can drive your car.

And I even went into your room and found the keys. So, I

could hang out with my friends at the game.

I knew he had been drinking so I took advantage of him. He didn't want to do but I kept begging him. So, he finally gave in.

When the game was over I went looking for him. I couldn't find him. So, I asked my friend's mother can I caught a ride home with them.

I thought maybe he went home and there I found him sleep. But your car wasn't parked in the driver's way. So, I went into the house and took a shower then jumped into my bed. Wait a minute so, who drove Bullet home? And who kept my car.

That is where I come in at. Lewis with a puzzle look on his face.

Now, who are you?

Oh, I'm also a Bullet friend too. I'm Jody and this is my friend Paul.

Okay, I don't understand.

Well, you might want to sit down for this.

As me and my friend Paul were walking back home from the same game. Bullet saw us and asked me if I would drive the car. Because he was drinking and he just wanted to go home.

So, I agree with too it. And he asked me to take another friend home. And I did as I was on my way to Bullet house. I hope he will be able to take me home.

A deer came from nowhere and I tried my best to miss it. But it was too late, I ended up hitting a big tree. And I was so scared, I jumped out of the car and ran home.

But the next morning I was getting ready for work. I turned on the news on the television. It was all on the news that someone had stolen a car. And leave the scene.

I tried to call Bullet and explain what I had done. But later I found out he was hiding.

So, I couldn't tell him what happened. Because he didn't want to get caught. And he is still on probation, and he might go to prison.

Oh, wow!

If I knew this wouldn't happen. Young girl, you know I'm going to get you back. I want you to feel the same as Bullet sitting there in jail. And he wonder if he is going to prison. Where killer and murdered don't mind do bad things to you.

So, Bailer if there was a law I could let my sister stay down here for a day or two.

To teach her a lesson about a lie can hurt.

Oh, by the way I will tell mom where you're at. And the reason why I done it is to my sweet lying sister. Lewis looked over at her with a very disappointed look on his face.

Bullet ran up to me and kissed me (Lewis) on the forehead and thanked me. Hey, wait a minute, don't thank me, your niece Selma did it!

Thank you God for giving another change to make things right. He yelled.

Man, when I get myself together. I will make some arrangements to help buy you another car.

No, that is not necessary.

Why?

Because Clover is going to get a part time job after school. Until she paid all the money that I put into my car.

That mean no more hanging out after school, no game, or friends come over to visit her. Plus, I'm going take her phone no more talking to anyone accept during school. And at the weekend she going to be at work. I hope this teach her not to lie again.

I'm now her personal driver back and forward to work. He folded his arms.

Wow, I don't be in Clover shoe, Selma shaking her head. A lie isn't worth losing everything. That could've got someone serious hurt or get kill over that lie. Now I hope you will remember this day. Don't do it anymore.

For that which I do I allow not: for what I would, that do I not; but what I hate, that do I.

If then I do that which I would not, I consent unto the law that it is good.

Now then it is no more I that do it. but sin that dwelleth in me.

For I know that in me (that is, in my flesh,) dwelleth no good thing: for to will is present with me, but how to perform that which is good I find not.

"For the good that I would I do not: but the evil which I

would not that I do.

Now if I do that would not, it is no more I that do it, but sin that dwelleth in me.

I find then a law, that, when I would do good, evil is present with me.

For I delight in the law of God after the inward man:

There is therefore now no condemnation to them which are in Christ Jesus, who walk not after the flesh, but after the Spirit.

For the law of the Spirit of life in Christ Jesus hath made me free from the law of sin and death.

For what the law could not do, in that it was weak through the flesh, God sending his own Son in the likeness of sinful flesh, and for sin, condemned sin in the flesh:

That the righteousness of the law might be fulfilled in us, who walk not after the flesh,

but after the Spirit.

For they that are after the flesh do mind the things of the flesh; but they that are after the Spirit the things of the Spirit.

For to be carnally minded is death; but to be spiritually minded is life and peace.

’That which was from the beginning, which we have heard, which we have seen with our eyes, which looked upon, and our hands have handled, of the Word of life;”

’’ (For the life was manifested, and we have seen it, and bear witness, and shew unto you that eternal life, which was with the Father, and was manifested unto us:)”

’’That which we have seen and heard declare we unto you, that ye also may have fellowship with us: and truly our fellowship is with the Father, and with his Son Jesus Christ.” ’’And these things write we unto you, that your joy may be full.”

’’Let not your heart be troubled: ye believe in God, believe also in me.”

’’In my Father’s house are many mansions: if it were not so, I would have told you. I go to prepare a place for you.”

’’And if I go and prepare a place for you, I will come again, and receive you unto myself; that where I am, there ye may be also.”

’’And whither I go ye know, and the way ye know.”

’’Thomas saith unto him, Lord, we know not whither thou goest; and how can we know the way?’’

"Jesus saith unto him I am the way, the truth, and the life: no man cometh unto the Father but by me."

"If ye had known me, ye should have known my Father also: and henceforth ye know him, and have seen him."

"I acknowledged my sin unto thee, and mine, iniquity have I not hid. I said, I will confess my transgressions unto the LORD; and thou forgavest the iniquity of my sin." Selah."

"For this shall every one that is godly pray unto thee in a time when thou mayest be found: surely in the floods of great waters they shall not come nigh unto him."

"Thou art my hiding place; thou shalt preserve me from trouble; thou shalt compass me about with songs of deliverance. Selah."

"I will instruct thee and teach thee in the way which thou shalt go: I will guide thee with mine eye."

Sinner Prayer

God love you
For God so loved the world, that he gave his only begotten son, that whosoever believeth in him should not perish, but have everlasting life.

John 3:16kjv

But God commendeth his love toward us, in that, while we were yet sinners, Christ died for us.

Romans 5:8kjv

All Are Sinner
''For all have sinned, and come short of the glory of God.''

Romans 3:23kjv

As it written, There is none righteous, no not one:

Romans 3:10kjv

God's Remedy for sin
For the wages of sin is death; but the gift of God is eternal life through Jesus Christ our Lord.

Romans 6:23kjv

But as many as received him, to them gave he power to become to sons of God, even to them that believe on his name:

John 1:12kjv

For I delivered unto you first of all that which I also received, that Christ died for our sins according to scriptures, and He was buried.

And that He rose the third day according to the scriptures.

1 Corinthians 15:3-4kjv

All May Be Saved now

Behold, I stand at the door and knock if anyone hear My voice and open the door, I will come in to him and dime with him and with me.

Revelation 3: 20kjv

For" whoever call on my name of the Lord shall be saved."

Romans 10:13kjv

Receive Christ As My Saviour

Confessing to God that I am a sinner, and believing that the Lord Jesus died for my sins on the cross and was raised for my justification. I do now receive and confess Him as my personal Saviour.

Assurance As a Believer

That if you confess with your mouth the Lord Jesus and believe in your heart that a God has raised Him from the dead, you will be saved.

Romans 10:9kjv

Most assuredly I say to you, he who hears My word and believes in Him who sent Me has everlasting life, and shall not coming into judgment, but has passed from death into life.

John 5:24kjv

But these are written that you may believe that Jesus in the Christ, the son of God, and that believing you may have in his name.

John 20:31kjv

All scripture is given by inspiration of God, and is profitable for doctrine, for reproof, of correction, instruction in righteousness:"

That the man of God may be perfect, throughly furnished unto all good works."

All scriptures taking from King James Version bible.

Thanks for your support and please share this book with your family and friends. If you like what you read please watch out. I have many more books coming to your bookstore. And my online at G&G bookstore.com.

Stony Harris

Author's Story

I born I Pickens County, Alabama, to John Earl Harris and late Minnie Bell Foster, as the youngest of ten children.

I was married to my Dorist L, Harris, and we raised four children. My writing journey began 2002 during the particularly Challenging period of my life.

I hit rock bottom, and forced me to confront and evaluate myself, and I didn't like what I saw. Then, led me to start attending church with my sister, over time, I found the church became an integral part of me.

I attend school at Bright Day Church in Christ. In Jeffersonville, Indiana 2007 I received my Christian Counselor license.

On May 27, 2016, I has the honor of becoming the first Deacon at New Destiny of Faith International Church in Louisville Kentucky.